05295

CHRISTIAN BELIEFS ABOUT LIFE AFTER DEATH

# SPCK Large Paperbacks

# CHRISTIAN BELIEFS
# ABOUT LIFE
# AFTER DEATH

Paul Badham

London
SPCK

First published 1976 by
The Macmillan Press Ltd
London and Basingstoke

First paperback edition 1978
SPCK
Holy Trinity Church
Marylebone Road
London NW1 4DU

Printed in Great Britain by
Billing & Sons Limited
Guildford, London and Worcester

ISBN 0 281 03601 2

# Contents

# Acknowledgements

I wish to thank Professor John Hick for his encouragement, guidance, help and friendship throughout the years of research which preceded this book. I also thank the parishioners of St Chad's Rubery, Birmingham, for enabling me to combine university research with a parochial ministry, and for impressing upon me the crucial significance of this topic for Christian faith today. My gratitude is also due to the students of St David's University College, Lampeter, discussions with whom greatly helped me in the task of re-writing the material of my doctoral thesis into the form of this present book, and in particular to Helen Orme and Gerald Parsons for reading the proofs, and the latter also for checking quotations. I also thank Mrs Myra Jones for typing the script so efficiently and promptly.

But my greatest debt is to my beloved wife Linda, who has helped at every stage of the book's development, and whose scientific learning, clarity of thought, and enthusiastic assistance have been of the utmost benefit to me.

P.B.

# Preface

My purpose in writing this book is to explore the foundations of Christian belief in life after death, to examine the ways in which this belief has been given expression, and to see whether it is tenable today.

In Part I, I consider how the religious faith of the Old Testament logically points forward towards a life beyond death and I seek to show how the Resurrection of Jesus came to be regarded as the foundation of the Christian Hope.

In Part II, I consider three versions of the doctrine of the Resurrection of the Body. I argue that any theory which postulates some kind of physical continuity between this existence and the next is no longer tenable, and that more sophisticated versions of what bodily resurrection means, in logic rely on some concept of a soul to ensure personal continuity.

In Part III, I defend the concept of the soul against contemporary materialist doctrines of man and seek to show the logical possibility of immortality.

P.B.

# Part I

# 1 The Contribution of the Old Testament to the Development of the Christian Hope

The Old Testament's understanding of death and immortality can be approached from two quite different positions. On the basis of its doctrine of man, any possibility of a future life would seem excluded. Yet in the light of its faith and trust in God, the Old Testament seems to point in a direction which must, and which did, lead to the development of a resurrection hope.

'We must all die. We are like water spilt on the grounds which cannot be gathered up again.'[1] 'Man will perish for ever like his own dung.'[2] He is 'of dust and will return to dust.'[3] In the grave he will rot away, 'with maggots beneath him and worms on top.'[4] Such is the Old Testament picture of the finality of death. It derives naturally from the Hebrew insistence that man is not an incarnate soul, but an animated body. He is an irreducibly physical being whose only possible life is on this earth and whose earthly life is bound up with the existence of the body.[5]

It is true that some passages speak of the soul departing at death,[6] or of the spirit returning to God,[7] but the consensus of Hebrew scholars is against any appeal to such passages as testimony of the immortality of the human spirit.[8] The primary meaning of *ruah*, or 'spirit' is the Spirit of God, the animating principle of all that lives.[9] Man like all other creatures,[10] comes to life only because God breathes into him his own breath.[11] This breath is on loan,[12] and when God withdraws it, the creature dies.[13] So, when Ecclesiastes says, 'Dust returns to the earth as it was, but the spirit returns to God who gave it',[14] he is not asserting the spirit's conquest of death, but only that God is taking back his own sustaining spirit. Similarly *nepes* or 'soul' basically means 'life, and what is more life bound up with a body'.[15] So when we are told that Rachel's *nepes* departed, this simply means that she died.[16] The Hebrew does not mean that her soul left her, as if it were something which could go off on its own.

The Old Testament places man completely within the natural order: 'He has no advantage over the beasts';[17] he is 'like the grass that withers, and the flowers that fade'.[18] In the presence of death man is less fortunate than the plants: 'There is always hope for a tree: when felled, it can start life again; its shoots continue to sprout . . . But man? He dies, and lifeless he remains . . . As a river shrinks and runs dry, so mortal man lies down never to rise . . . as a rain storm scours soil from the soil, so you wipe out the hope of frail man . . . and he is gone.'[19] 'In that same hour all his thinking ends;'[20] 'The dead know nothing, they have no more reward; but the memory of them is lost.'[21]

Most of these quotations come from the Psalms, Ecclesiastes, and Job and represent a developed stage in Hebrew thought. Earlier data is more ambiguous. According to R.H. Charles, the Hebrews inherited a concept of Sheol as an abode of shadowy dead, situated deep beneath the earth, from the time when they lived in the valley of the Euphrates and shared this and other beliefs with the contemporary Babylonians.[22] As Yahwism developed, death came to be thought of as total extinction, and the word 'Sheol' came to be used simply as a poetic way of talking about the Grave as the ultimate destiny for all mankind.[23] Since however the Old Testament writings derive from widely diverse periods of thought one can never be sure whether any particular reference to Sheol should be understood as a poetic description of the dead in their graves, or as a reference to a shadowy survival in a supposed underworld. What is certain is that Sheol was never regarded as offering any kind of worthwhile, significant, or personal life, and that in developed Yahwism death came to be equated with cessation of being.

This explicit denial of life after death seems a strange starting point for the development of such a hope, yet it may have been an essential first step. Charles argues that belief in Sheol had to be rooted out before any worthwhile concept of a future life could be formulated.

> The nature of existence in Sheol was heathen and non-moral, and could in no sense form a basis on which to found an ethical and spiritual doctrine of the future life. Thus the first stage was .. eminently destructive in character, but this only with a view to a higher reconstruction. For whilst Yahwism was destroying the false life in Sheol it was steadily developing in the individual the consciousness of a new life and a new worth through immediate communion with God. Now it is from the consciousness of this new life, and not from any moribund existence in Sheol, that the doctrine of a blessed future — whether of the soul only immediately after death, or of the soul and body through a resurrection at some later date — was developed in Israel. Thus this doctrine was a new creation, the offspring of faith in God on the part of Israel's saints.[24]

Old Testament scholarship endorses this proposition that the subsequent faith in a future life was derived from reflection on the quality of the individual's relationship with God, as described by the Old Testament writers and as experienced by the faithful believer.[25] The Old Testament is clear that there is nothing in man or nature, and nothing that man can do, that could provide any grounds for hoping for a life after death. Yahweh alone is the Lord of Life: 'In his hand is the life of every living thing and the breath of all mankind.'[26] Yet if man can really enter into a personal relationship with God and if Yahweh is truly Lord of all life, it follows that he can rescue his faithful from the power of death itself.

Legends of outstanding individuals escaping death go far back into Israel's history in the mysterious accounts of the ascension of Elijah and the translation of Enoch.[27] Few today would regard these stories as historical, yet in these primitive legends we can see a foreshadowing of the beliefs and values which were later to form the basis for future hope. Thus Enoch was 'translated' because 'he walked with God',[28] perhaps suggesting that this unknown saint was thought to enjoy a relationship with God too strong for death to sever.

Likewise Elijah's experience of God as 'a still small voice'[29] might suggest that a deeply personal awareness of God lay at the heart of Elijah's faith.[30] Notice too the strong sense of Elijah's distinctive individuality. We are given no details of his tribe, background or family, and we are frequently told that he felt himself to be utterly isolated, 'I, even I only, am left.'[31] Not till others shared in both his faith and sense of individual identity did the general expectation of a future life develop.

Most scholars identify the change towards an individualistic understanding of religion with the New Covenant described in the 31st chapter of Jeremiah. E.W. Heaton describes this as an 'extraordinarily new conception' of what man's relationship to God should be.[32] Charles thinks that the significance of this New Covenant lies in its establishing a relationship between God and the individual which 'would supersede the old relation which had existed between Yahweh and the nation as a whole ... Henceforth the individual would step into the place of the nation in its relation to Yahweh, and the individual would henceforth constitute the religious unit.'[33]

This overstates the case, for Jeremiah says that the covenant would be made 'with the house of Israel and the house of Judah'.[34] However, commentators seem agreed that the passage insists that authentic knowledge of God must be based on first hand experience, personally true for each member of the community.[35] For Jeremiah a man is not a follower of God simply because of his membership of the Jewish race,[36] nor because he had book knowledge of the religious traditions of his people,[37] or because he participates in worship,[38] or reverences the Temple.[39] It is not these externals which matter to Jeremiah, but only an unmediated awareness of God.[40] Charles writes, 'Jeremiah was the first to conceive religion as the communion of the individual soul with God' so that 'each individual enters into the privileges of the prophet.'[41]

In the writings of Ezekiel this stress on the importance of the individual and the essentially personal nature of religion was further developed and became 'firmly rooted in the national consciousness.'[42] One of the most important con-

sequences of this was that it came to be believed that
punishment or reward could only appropriately be visited on
the individual offender. 'The man who has sinned is the one
who must die; a son is not to suffer for the sins of his father,
nor a father for the sins of his son. To the upright man his
integrity will be credited, to the wicked his wickedness.'[43] In
saying this Ezekiel was not recommending guidelines for the
fair administration of human justice, rather he was affirming
his faith in a divine justice, manifesting itself through the
circumstances of everyday life. This faith found expression in
the Book of Proverbs and the Psalter, both of which provide
any number of examples of how this was believed to operate:

> Unbelievers suffer want and go hungry,
> but those who seek the Lord lack no good thing.[44]

> Evildoers will be destroyed,
> but they who hope in the Lord shall possess the land.[45]

> For you the Lord is a safe retreat; . . .
> No disaster shall befall you,
> No calamity shall come upon your home.[46]

> Misfortune pursues sinners,
> but prosperity rewards the righteous.[47]

> The righteous has enough to satisfy his appetite,
> but the belly of the wicked suffers want.[48]

> The righteous is delivered from trouble,
> and the wicked gets into it instead.[49]

This idea of a direct relationship between virtue and
prosperity on the one hand, and wickedness and disaster on
the other arose through taking the Prophetic and Deutero-
nomic concept of God's judgement in history, and applying
it, not to nations but to individuals. There are serious
difficulties about thus re-applying the doctrine. Professor
Herbert Butterfield has shown that a very strong case can be
made for the idea of divine judgement in history,[50] but he
points out that 'The moral judgements of history are often
long-term affairs, so that one gets the impression that the sins
of the fathers are visited on the children to the third and
fourth generation.'[51] He suggests for instance that although

Frederick the Great and Bismarck enjoyed remarkable success in their own life-times through their use of military power, 'I do not think we are interpolating anything fanciful into the structure of history, if we say that . . . in 1918 . . . or in 1945 . . . a judgement has been passed on the militarism of Prussia . . . [although] it was not a judgement that fell on Frederick the Great and Bismarck personally.'[52] Thus the outstanding modern champion of the idea of a moral order in history explicitly rules out the appropriateness of re-applying the concept to the individual.

Within the Old Testament both Job and Ecclesiastes protest against the idea that during the life-time of the individual person 'he who sows goodness reaps a sure reward.'[53] while 'he who sows injustice reaps trouble.'[54] These proverbs are too often false to the facts of life. Ecclesiastes comments cynically, 'In my empty existence I have seen it all, from a righteous man perishing in his righteousness to a wicked man growing old in his wicked-ness.'[55] And Job asks 'How often is the lamp of the wicked snuffed out? and how often does ruin come upon them?'[56] He observes that 'The wicked enjoy long life, hale in old age and great and powerful. They live to see their children settled . . . their families secure and safe; . . . Their lives close in prosperity, and they go down to Sheol in peace.'[57]

Neither Job nor Ecclesiastes can reconcile their experience of life with the idea of divine justice being done to the individual. So Ecclesiastes denies the concept, 'Good man and sinner fare alike . . . This is what is wrong with all that is done here under the sun.'[58] Job ends by concluding that the mystery passes man's understanding and he has no right to question the wisdom of his creator: 'I have spoken of great things which I have not understood, things too wonderful for me to know.'[59]

It is not surprising that they came to these conclusions for if one believes that death is the end, then there is simply no way belief in divine justice for the individual can be reconciled with life as we experience it. Professor John Hick has shown in his "Evil and the God of Love" that 'if there is any eventual resolution of the interplay between good and evil, . . . it must lie beyond . . . the enigma of death. Therefore we cannot hope to state a Christian theodicy without taking seriously the doctrine of a life beyond the grave.'[60]

This is what the religious thinkers of Israel found. As long as God's concern was thought to be with the nation as a whole, it was possible to believe in a divine justice working through history without any concept of a future life for the individual members of that nation. But once religion was seen as the relationship between man and his maker, then the old theodicy collapsed. After optimism about the fairness of life had been exposed as false, it came to be seen that belief in divine justice for the individual required belief in a future life, and was negated by its absence. Recognising this, Ecclesiastes 'gave himself up to despair.'[61] while Job speculated wistfully, but hopelessly about a recall from the grave:

If only you would hide me in Sheol
and shelter me there until your anger is past,
fixing a certain day for calling me to mind —
for once a man is dead can he come back to life? —
day after day of my service I would wait
for my relief to come.
Then you would call, and I should answer,
you would see the work of your hand once more . . .

But no! you destroy man's hope.
You crush him once for all and he is gone.[62]

According to Charles, 'what appears only as an impassioned desire [in the passage cited above] rises into a real, though possibly only momentary conviction in Chapter 19, verses 25—27.'[63] The Revised Standard Version translates this passage as follows:

I know that my Redeemer lives,
and at last he will stand upon the earth;
and after my skin has been thus destroyed,
then without my flesh I shall see God,
whom I shall see on my side,
and my eyes shall behold and not another.

Professor William Irwin writes that there is 'no doubt that the RSV is right; Job affirms his conviction that after death he will see God.'[64] R.H. Charles comments 'Job declares that

God will appear for his vindication, and that after his death (i.e. without the body) he shall witness this vindication, and enjoy the vision of God. But we cannot infer that this divine experience will endure beyond the moment of Job's justification by God. It is not the blessed immortality of the departed soul that is referred to here, but its actual entrance into and enjoyment of the higher life, however momentary its duration.'[65] This view is endorsed by T.H. Robinson who comments, 'All that concerns Job is to know that death will not cut him off from God.' Robinson thinks that this newly found faith expressed here 'is pivotal in man's spiritual destiny. The supreme barrier to a conception of eternal life ... is the fact of death. Till men see that death is no longer an impassable barrier, there can be no advance towards belief in full immortality ... Job opened a door through which later generations could pass, and reach a picture of an eternal life which is a true counterpart of the eternal God.'[66]

The Jerusalem Bible translation says that Job will see God 'from his flesh ... after his awakening' The New English Bible translates it thus: 'In my heart I know that my vindicator lives, and that he will rise last to speak in court: and I shall discern my witness standing at my side and see my defending counsel, even God himself, whom I shall see with my own eyes, I myself and no other.' This appears to refer to a vindicating vision of God, and the translation does not indicate whether this vision would occur, before, at, or after death. Professor H.H. Rowley analyses the contrasting views of twenty-six scholars and concludes, 'While it must be agreed that the words are ambiguous, I think it is possible that the author is here reaching out after something more satisfying than the dreary doctrine of Sheol reflected elsewhere in his book. But he has not securely grasped it.'[67]

This conclusion seems fair. Job's reflections on the inequities of life coupled with his belief in a just and righteous God impel him towards the idea that death cannot be the end of the matter. In Job's case this idea was nothing more than a momentary spark of hope kindled by an intense longing, for Job's normative view seems expressed in his lament that 'my days are swifter than a weaver's shuttle, and come to an end without hope.'[68] Nevertheless the chain of thought which for a moment lifted Job above his despair was ultimately to triumph in the last days of the Old Testament period when the problem of innocent suffering became inescapable.

In settled times there is often a sufficient correlation between the virtues of diligence, thrift, and honesty, and subsequent material prosperity for healthy and prosperous men of virtue to close their eyes to the fact of innocent suffering. But the bankruptcy of such a view reveals itself when the whole fabric of society is shattered, and when rich and poor, good and bad, are equally submerged in the ruins of their shared civilisation. Professor Eichrodt writes, 'It is no accident that the extant passages which do speak of a resurrection even of the individual believer manifestly come from times of great crisis. Both the little apocalypse of Isaiah 24—27 and the book of Daniel are the products of periods when severe tribulations were having a profoundly convulsive impact, the former from the time when "the birth-pangs of a new era created an age of neurotic anxiety" after the victorious career of Alexander the Great and the setting up of the kingdoms of the Diadochi, the latter from the period of intense persecution under Antiochus Epiphanes. Both strive for certainty and clarity with regard to God's final plan, and find comfort in the vision of the final victory of the kingdom of God over all the powers of the world.'[69] In the history of thought the affirmation of resurrection in Isaiah 26/19 is an isolated affirmation which was not then taken up into Israel's religious tradition, whereas the reference to a future life in Daniel 12/1 ff. comes from the precise period when resurrection hope emerged as a normative belief.

According to Professor John Bright

The ancestors of the later Pharisees, were driven to embrace [belief in a future life] because only so could the justice of God, which they refused to question, be harmonized with the facts of experience. The persecutions of Antiochus undoubtedly cast the deciding vote. As righteous men were brutally done to death, or lost their lives fighting for the faith, belief that God would vindicate his justice beyond the grave became an absolute necessity for the majority of Jews. In the second century and after, as we see from I Enoch, the Testaments of the Twelve Patriarchs, and other writings, belief in a general resurrection and a final judgement gained the upper hand. It was a new doctrine, but it was one that was needed to fill out the structure of Israel's faith, if that faith was to remain tenable. Though Sadducees never acquiesced in it . . . it became an accepted belief among Jews and was triumphantly reaffirmed in the Christian Gospel.[70]

So far I have explored one consequence of the reapplication of Israel's Covenant faith from the nation to the individual. I have argued that if one believes that God really will see justice done for the individual, then the fact of innocent suffering demands, and the martyrdom of the believer requires, belief in a future life. But another consequence of the rise of individualism equally points in this direction, namely that the individual worshipper comes to believe that he is, as an individual, in a relationship with God which death cannot sever.

Part of Job's revulsion against his fate stemmed from his sense that death not only threatened his belief in God's justice, but also made a mockery of his belief that God had a purpose in creating him, and implied that God was merely dissembling in seeming to enter into a personal relationship with him.

> Your own hands shaped me, modelled me;
> and would you now have second thoughts and destroy
> me?[71]

> Did you not . . . clothe me with skin and flesh,
> and weave me of bone and sinew?
> And then you endowed me with life,
> watched each breath of mine with tender care.
> Yet after all, you were dissembling.[72]

What baffled Job was that 'I, whom God has fostered father-like from childhood, and guided since I left my mother's womb',[73] should now be doomed to extinction, in spite of the fact that 'I have walked in his way without swerving; . . . cherishing the words from his mouth in my breast.'[74] Indeed Job pleads with God to remember the closeness of their relationship, pointing out that if the relationship matters to God then God will miss Job if he allows him to collapse into nothingness:

It will not be long before I lie in the earth;
then you will look for me, but I shall be no more.[75]

Ecclesiastes saw this same truth but from quite a different perspective. His starting point was belief in death as final extinction, and from this premise he deduced that 'man is a creature of chance';[76] that 'no one knows' whether God's attitude is one of 'love or hatred';[77] that life is devoid of any ultimate purpose;[78] that man 'has no comprehension of God's work from beginning to end';[79] that there is 'nothing good for man except to be happy and live the best life he can while he is alive[80] ... and enjoy life with a woman [he] loves all the days of [his] alloted span here under the sun, empty as they are.'[82]

What Job and Ecclesiastes both see from their differing viewpoints are these truths: if man is purposefully created by an all-powerful God, and if man can enjoy a personal relationship with God which God values, and if each man as a unique individual really matters to the all-powerful and all-loving God, then God simply will not allow that individual and that relationship to be destroyed finally by death. Alternatively if death really is the end, then man cannot ultimately matter to God. The question to be decided is whether one feels that Job's momentary conviction of the certainty of a future life was a truer insight into reality than either Job's normative pessimism or Ecclesiastes' view that 'it is better to be satisfied with what is before your eyes than give free rein to desire.'[83]

The way each person decides in his own mind about the issue probably depends upon whether or not he believes that he has himself had experience of entering a personal relationship with God. This may seem an exceedingly frail basis upon which to build so momentous a hope as the expectation of a future life, but the basis will seem in fact as strong, or as weak, or as non-existent, as the individual's own religious experiences have been. For in the final analysis our judgements concerning religious truths are intimately linked to the quality of experiences which we have enjoyed.

Professor John Hick has pointed out in another context that 'It is in principle quite possible for one person to have participated in experiences on the basis of which it is reasonable for him to believe in God and even unreasonable not to, while another person who has not participated in those experiences may equally reasonably not believe in God.'[84] I am extending this argument and saying that if a person has had experiences which convince him that there is indeed a loving God, and that he himself has truly entered into a loving relationship with this God, then it may be reasonable for such a man to believe that God will hold him in being beyond the grave, while for one who has had no such experiences, this argument for a future life will seem wholly vacuous.

If we turn back to the Old Testament and look at the Psalms which express the deepest awareness of a personal relationship with God, we find in them expressions of such utter trust and so strong a sense of communion with God that belief in a future life seems an inevitable consequence. As D.S. Russell says, 'There is certainly no clearly defined doctrine of an after-life set forth in these passages; and yet the hope expressed is such that it can reach its logical conclusion only in the acceptance of such a belief.'[85]

Psalm 16/8 affirms utter confidence in God,

I have set the Lord continually before me;
with him at my right hand I cannot be shaken.

Confidence in a future life is a corollary of such utter faith:

Therefore my heart exults
and my spirit rejoices,
my body too rests unafraid;
for thou wilt not abandon me to Sheol
nor suffer thy faithful servant to see the pit.
Thou wilt show me the path of life;
in thy presence is the fullness of joy,
in thy right hand pleasures for evermore.[86]

Professor Weiser comments that 'the great majority of more recent expositors hold the view that what the author has in mind is that God will protect him from a sudden, untimely, or evil death. However, neither the wording of the verse nor the general circumstances and attitude of the poet suggest such an interpretation . . . There is no reason to doubt that the poet has in mind . . . death as such . . . and by virtue of his faith in God he is progressing towards the conquest of the fear of death in his heart.'[87] Weiser points out the psalmist gives no clue as to how he thinks death will be overcome. 'The fact that death has been overcome by God is the firm foundation which enables the poet to envisage death with an assurance that does not doubt, whereas the question of "how" God will achieve that goal remains a divine mystery which is still concealed. There is one thing which he knows however: "Thou wilt show me the path of life" . . . a life lived in communion with God which will be carried on even after death.'[88] This interpretation of the psalm is endorsed by Professor G.W. Anderson who writes that 'The psalmist holds that communion with God is the supreme good; and this is a central element in the final biblical view of life after death.'[89]

In Psalm 49 the poet asserts that 'men are like oxen whose life cannot last',[90] and that the wealth of the rich and self-assured will not help them to escape this fate. Nevertheless the poet is convinced that,

God will ransom my life,
he will take me from the power of Sheol.[91]

Charles suggests that this psalm teaches that 'Sheol is the future abode of the wicked only; heaven is that of the righteous.'[92] This probably gives too systematic an account of the writer's throught. Weiser is probably closer to the poet's thought when he describes it thus: 'Because in the poet's view it is not perishable earthly possessions which determine the importance of man's life but the fact that he lives his life in God, the death which he will have to suffer eventually does not have for him the dreadful significance of a breaking down of everything which is valuable in life; for death is transcended by the power of his God, who is able to redeem him from the power of death. And it is this relationship to God which in his view represents man's true life. This is why he may cherish the hope that God will indeed redeem him from death and, by "receiving"[93] him, will hereafter establish a living communion between himself and the poet which will be even more intimate than the one which already exists at present'[94]

Finally let us turn to Psalm 73 which H. Wheeler Robinson describes as the 'most notable' of those which point towards a future life,[95] and which Gottwald describes as venturing near 'the affirmation that death will not destroy his intimate relation with God.'[96] What the Psalmist says is:

> I am always with thee,
> thou holdest my right hand;
> thou dost guide me by the counsel
> and afterward wilt receive me with glory.
> Whom have I in heaven but thee?
> And having thee, I desire nothing else on earth.
> Thou heart and body fail,
> Yet God is my possession for ever . . .
> My chief good is to be near thee, O God;
> I have chosen thee, Lord God, to be my refuge.[97]

According to Charles the message is that 'the highest blessedness of the righteous consists in unbroken communion with God — unbroken even by death; for after this life God takes them to himself.'[98] As Weiser puts it, 'Faith overcomes death in the light of the eternal presence of God.'[99]

It does seem to me these psalms we have considered do affirm a basis on which faith in a future life can be built. Eichrodt sums up the situation thus:

> The common factor linking all these witnesses to the conquest of death in the life of the individual is that their certainty is built on the gift of fellowship with God here and now. Because God has spoken to Man, and still speaks, he is therefore lifted out of the compulsion of mortality and sees before him the path of life. No eternal substance in Man asserts itself against death, no attribute of his spiritual being bestowed upon him at his creation assures

him of immortality; . . . [in Luther's words] "Where, however, or with whom, God speaks, whether in wrath or in grace, the same is certainly immortal. The Person of the God who speaks, and the Word of God show that we are creatures with whom God wills to speak even unto eternity and in an immortal manner."[100]

In conclusion we may say that when the Old Testament looks at man it concludes that he cannot live beyond the grave, but when it looks towards God, and ponders over the relationship between God and man it moves in a direction which must, and which did, lead men towards a future hope. Wheeler Robinson puts this well: 'The faith of the Old Testament logically points forward towards a life beyond death, because it is so sure of an inviolable fellowship with God, but . . . it does not attain to any clear vision of the goal of its journey. Nevertheless this religious faith supplied the real content for the resurrection hope when this had been reached.'[101]

# 2 The Significance of Jesus' Resurrection

In his first letter to the Corinthians, St Paul writes, 'I must remind you of the Gospel that I preached to you; the Gospel which you received, on which you have taken your stand, and which is now bringing you salvation.'[1] He goes on to declare that this Gospel consists 'first and foremost' in the news of Jesus' resurrection. This was the distinctive and original Gospel message, for as Paul tells his converts, 'I handed on to you the facts which had been imparted to me.' William Neil explains its importance thus:

> The Christian Church was not founded on the teaching of Jesus. It was founded by men who believed that the Jesus whom they had forsaken to go to his death alone had risen from the grave triumphant over death, that he had appeared to them, and thereby had turned the cross from being a symbol of shame and defeat into a gateway to victory and glory. Not only was the Church founded on this belief, but the whole of the New Testament was written as a result of it.[2]

For this reason Archbishop Ramsey argues that 'The Resurrection is a true starting point for the study and meaning of the New Testament.'[3]

Jesus' resurrection had this importance because it was never regarded as simply the deliverance from death of one righteous individual as a believing Jew might have looked on the ascension of Enoch, Elijah, or Moses.[4] Instead it was thought of as having universal significance as the clue to what we ourselves may expect to happen after our death: 'For as in Adam all die, so in Christ shall all be made alive.'[5] It is therefore important to discover whether belief in Jesus' resurrection has a reliable historical foundation and what the nature of his resurrection was.

But is the resurrection open to historical investigation? Not according to Karl Barth. For him the resurrection 'cannot be thought of as history.'[6] As 'an autonomous new act of God',[7] it contains 'no component of human action'[8] and as such transcends history. Nevertheless Barth believes the resurrection was a real event: 'It happened in the same sense as the crucifixion happened, in the human sphere and in human time, as an actual event within the world with an objective content.'[9] Barth's difficulty is that he wants to preserve the objectivity of the resurrection, but at the same time he feels with Günther Bornkamn that 'Faith cannot and should not be dependent on the change and uncertainty of historical research.'[10] Consequently, while maintaining that the resurrection really happened, he insists that historical inquiry is not a valid way of checking its credentials.

I believe that this position is untenable. Professor D.M. Mackinnon explains why: 'If the tomb was empty, there must have been a moment in time when the body of Jesus was in the tomb, and a moment afterwards when it was not. And if we say this . . . we are . . . putting ourselves in bondage to the settlement of questions which are questions of historical fact.'[11] As William Lillie says, 'There is no difference in principle between the fact of a tomb being empty in *AD* 29, and the fact of a test-tube being empty in 1965.'[12] The same argument applies to the reported appearances of Jesus. If these happened, they happened in history. Even if the resurrection were no more than 'a rise of faith in the risen Lord'[13] on the part of Jesus' disciples, then this change in them also happened in history. A faith which claims that something which happened in the past is important cannot evade historical scrutiny of that claim.

Heinz Zahrnt disputes the possibility of historical inquiry into the resurrection on the grounds that there is no direct evidence available. 'The historian cannot verify that Jesus rose from the dead . . . He can only verify that Peter and the other disciples maintained that Jesus had risen and had appeared to them.'[14] Moreover although Zahrnt believes that 'the report of the empty tomb ... must be allowed to stand'[15] he argues that 'In no event is belief in the resurrection of Jesus to be supported by belief in the empty tomb, for this is simply to guarantee one belief by reference to another.'[16]

Professor W. Marxsen develops this, arguing that in the case of the empty tomb, 'We have to do with a historical fact which not only can be interpreted differently, but also has been interpreted differently. It can be claimed that the disciples stole the corpse, that is why the tomb is empty. But it can also be claimed that Jesus is risen, and that is why the tomb is empty ... It is not possible to check the correctness of the [differing] interpretations ... It is therefore not permissible ... to speak of the event of Jesus' resurrection, because it is not permissible to turn an interpretation into an objective fact.'[17] Similarly with the appearances of Jesus, Marxsen claims: 'In historical terms it can only be established ... that witnesses, after the death of Jesus, claimed that something had happened to them which they described as seeing Jesus, and reflection on this experience led them to the interpretation that Jesus had been raised from the dead.'[18]

Marxsen's point is that we have no right to claim as an event something which is only one possible way of interpreting the available historical data. He feels this to be a fundamental principle of historical inquiry and insists that theologians 'must simply acknowledge that the scientific study of history has its own methodology.'[19] But is Marxsen's analysis correct? He gives no evidence to support his claim that, 'It is not possible to check the correctness of the differing interpretations', so presumably he is thinking only in terms of the impossibility of achieving 100 per cent certainty over a historical question for which more than one answer is logically possible. But is this realistic? I suggest that most modern historians are fully aware of the relativity of virtually all their judgements and see their task not as the achievement of certainty, but of establishing what seems to them to be the most probable interpretation.

In an article on 'The Methodology of History' in the 1971 *Encyclopaedia Britannica*, Dr C.F. Slade contrasts modern historical methodology with the 'impossible "objective" or "scientific" history of the later 19th Century.'[20] He writes, 'The occurrences themselves can never be experienced by the historian. What he has at his disposal are either accounts of occurrences as seen by contemporaries or something, be it verbal, written, or material that is the end product of an occurrence . . . these "traces" are the "facts" of history, the actual occurrences are deductions from the facts.' The primary source of materials for the historian 'Consists of events as seen through the eyes of an individual and therefore as interpreted by him.' A similar point of view is expressed in the guidance given to schoolboys thinking about reading History at an English University in the book *Which University?*: 'The most important difference between the study of history at School and at University is that it becomes much more of a critical interpretative study of the past rather than just an amassing of information.'[21]

Thus modern historical study — as distinct from later 19th Century or school-boy historical study — sees that human judgement and interpretation of the data play a very significant part in establishing the likelihood or otherwise of alleged past events. We cannot therefore dismiss the question of the historicity of the resurrection of Jesus simply because it is to be deduced from other historical data. The question is whether or not it is a reasonable deduction to make.

Let us start by considering the most certain facts about Jesus: that he was crucified, and that the early Church proclaimed him as risen. The crucifixion is the best evidenced fact about Jesus, being attested to by some of the earliest opponents of Christianity: Tacitus, the Roman historian writing in AD 110, says 'Christ was crucified by the procurator Pontius Pilate during the reign of Tiberius Caesar';[22] Celsus, a Greek philosopher writing in the early 2nd Century attacking Christianity, adds his witness to the crucifixion, and sees the degradation of this death as an important argument against faith in Christ;[23] The Jewish Talmud declares that Jesus was 'a rabbi who led Israel astray' and that he was executed on the eve of the Passover.[24] Thus the first Christians and their first opponents unite in affirming his crucifixion. The Koran's denial of the Crucifixion need not concern us here, since it is based on much later docetic sources, and in fact itself affirms that the sensory evidence was that Jesus was crucified: 'The Jews ... did not ... crucify him, but it was made to appear that way to them.'[25] This docetic hypothesis, that by a miracle God made it appear to the Jews that they were crucifying Jesus, whereas in reality God had taken him to himself, is most unlikely to appeal today. Yet this is the only alternative to a historic crucifixion put forward in the first eighteen hundred years of the Church's life. It seems therefore that there are very strong grounds for believing in the historic crucifixion. Indeed, David Jenkins argues that the evidence is so strong that no reasonable man acquainted with it can deny it.[26]

The evidence for the second historical fact that the first Christians came to believe that Jesus had risen is even stronger, namely the New Testament documents. For whatever else the New Testament may be, it is at least a record of what the early Christians believed; and that Jesus had risen from the dead is the perspective which dominates all the New Testament. From the New Testament and from the early Christian writings which followed, it becomes clear that the central message of the first Christians was that Jesus had risen. We know that they passionately believed in the resurrection message which they preached, for they were able to persuade others to share their belief, and were even prepared to die as witnesses to it. Unless the disciples themselves had been totally convinced that Jesus had risen, I do not think they would have been able to persuade so many others to share belief in so incredible a claim. Further, only men who are wholly convinced of the validity of their beliefs are prepared to die as witnesses to it. The word 'martyr' is the Greek for 'witness' and was used explicitly for those Christians who died as witnesses to the resurrection. Hence from the writings, the preaching, the success in converting others, and the faithfulness to death of the first disciples, I think it is reasonable to assert that their Easter Faith is a historical fact.

Further to these historical considerations I am also impressed by a psychological fact about mourning to which

Dr Murray Parkes has drawn attention. He says of mourning 'I know of no other psychological illness which follows so stereotyped and predictable a course.' He reports that there is a tendency for the bereaved to become numb, for their emotions to be blunted, and for them to be 'shut in on themselves.'[27] Applying this to the disciples after Jesus' death we see this pattern followed to the letter.[28] But suddenly it was broken. The disciples became changed men boldly proclaiming that Jesus had risen. What caused this change? The disciples' own explanation was that Jesus had risen and appeared to them. Many are convinced that this is the only explanation which will do justice to the data. But is this necessarily so?

Don Cupitt regards the argument I have outlined above as saying, 'How could a world-conquering faith have begun among defeated, hopeless men unless the resurrection-faith were true?' To which he responds, 'Any sociologist could reply, it is precisely among the powerless that such beliefs begin.'[29] He supports this by pointing out that in 1969, when he was writing his book, left-wing students were displaying posters which said 'Che lives!' in defiance of the fact that he had been killed in the previous year. He also mentions similar claims made by Black Muslims in 1918, and Iron Guard Fascists in 1940, about their dead leaders.[30] However I suggest that the fact that students no longer adorn their rooms with Che posters is sufficient to refute the alleged parallels.

I accept that hopeless, defeated, or bereaved persons often delude themselves and refuse to accept their true position. But there is all the difference in the world between the tearful moan, 'I simply can't believe that he's dead', and the confident proclamation, 'God has raised this man to life.'[31] One sympathises with the illusions of those whose hopes have been crushed, but one is not thereby persuaded to share them. The historical issue involved in the resurrection claim is not why the disciples continued to cling to a false belief that Jesus was still alive, but why they acquired a radically new belief that he had risen.

My argument for regarding the resurrection of Jesus as a real event moves from the fact of the disciples' faith to the need for some sufficient cause to account for it. Bultmann however disputes this procedure. He suggests that 'the resurrection narratives, and every other mention of the resurrection in the New Testament, be understood simply as an attempt to convey the meaning of the cross.'[32] It follows from this that for Bultmann 'Faith in the resurrection is really the same thing as faith in the saving efficacy of the cross,'[33] and consequently no objective resurrection is required. My difficulty with this position is that for me the cross without its sequel would seem a symbol not of man's salvation but of his abandonment.

Let Professor Lampe remind us of the position as the disciples might have seen it after the crucifixion:

> Here was one whose whole life was grounded in trust in God: in the certainty that God is good; that he can be called 'Father' — and not only by Jesus himself but also by all those who learn to say 'Our Father'. Here was one who was ready to accept people as they were, with all their unlovableness, understand them, and make them his friends; one who met hatred with love and forgiveness; one who showed up the selfishness of complacent people, condemned it and made them begin to hate it too; one who so moved people that they changed their whole outlook and became his followers. His love and forgiveness extended to everyone except those who were wilfully blind to it. It included even those who murdered him. And he believed that in all this he was speaking and acting with the authority of God; that this was the real truth about the way things are.
>
> But it wasn't. That Friday was the end. God, if there was a God, had turned away. The life of Jesus had proved to be a catastrophic mockery: one of those great ironical jokes that history sometimes plays with the best of men. Jesus died with the cry 'My God, my God, why hast thou forsaken me',[34] — the only time Jesus did not call God 'Father'.[35]

How could the disciples have regained their confidence in Jesus' teaching after that? If Jesus' death was the end, then his preaching about the character of God and the nature of life was simply false, and nothing could justify the disciples in continuing to perpetrate such falsehood. Without a message of hope concerning Jesus, the disciples could not for one moment have convinced themselves or others that he was truly the Christ. As William Neil says, 'A crucified Messiah was so complete a travesty of all that had ever been hoped for and promised that Jesus' claim to be what the prophets foretold would never have been countenanced for a week, let alone two thousand years, if the cross had been the end.'[36]

Hence I conclude that a Resurrection-Faith requires a Resurrection-Event. If, as Bultmann says, the rise of the Easter faith was the 'self-attestation of the risen Lord,'[37] then it would seem to me to be logically necessary that this 'risenness' of the Lord was an actual reality, and that his 'self-attestation' should truly attest to his personal aliveness. But what was the nature of this resurrection? What were the disciples affirming when they talked of Jesus rising and appearing to them?

The earliest written evidence we possess as to how the first Christians understood the resurrection comes from 1 Corinthians 15. In this St Paul cites what appears to be an 'official list' of the appearances of Jesus: 'I handed on to you the facts which had been imparted to me: that Christ died for our sins, in accordance with the scriptures; that he was buried; that he was raised to life on the third day, according to the scriptures; that he appeared to Cephas, and afterwards to the Twelve. Then he appeared to over five hundred of our brothers at once, most of whom are still alive, though some have died. Then he appeared to James, and afterwards to all the apostles. In the end he appeared even to me.'[38]

One of the most interesting features of this list is that Paul should append his own experience to something which looks like an authoritative list of the original resurrection appearances of Jesus. This strongly suggests that Paul regarded his experience on the Damascus road as being of the same type as the experiences of the first apostles, and consequently if we explore the nature of Paul's own experience we may gain an insight into how the resurrection appearances of Jesus were originally understood by the first Christians.

St Paul describes his experience as 'a revelation' (Galatians,

1/16), 'a seeing' (1 Corinthians 9/1), and 'an appearance' (1 Corinthians 15/8). In the account in Acts 26/19 which, though later, probably still represents a valid tradition, Paul describes it as 'a heavenly vision'. This seems quite significant, particularly when we recall that the word *'opthe'*, which Paul uses to describe the appearances of Jesus to his disciples, is the word commonly used to denote an appearance of God, or of God's angel.[39] This suggests that Paul regarded the appearances of Jesus as visionary experiences rather than objective seeings. This would seem supported by the terminology he uses in Galations 1/16 where he says, 'God revealed his Son to me', or in a literal translation 'in me', suggesting perhaps an inward experience. Moreover the three accounts in Acts of Paul's experience seem to imply that it was an inward vision rather than an external happening, for although the reports are confused and contradictory, they all state that Paul's companions did not fully share in his experience.[40]

Turning to the Gospels we find that in all the accounts there is something unusual about the appearances of Jesus. In Matthew there is a highly coloured account of an appearance to the guards and then to the women at the tomb;[41] then there is an account of an appearance to Jesus' disciples in which we are told that 'when they saw him they worshipped him; but some doubted.'[42] This is perhaps the strongest evidence for the inward nature of Jesus' appearances, for a physical appearance, such as a camera might have recorded, would have left no room for this doubt. In Luke there is the story of the road to Emmaus where two disciples were joined by a Jesus they did not recognise and who vanished from their home at the moment of recognition;[43] then there is an appearance of Jesus to the twelve in which he suddenly appeared among them, ate and talked with them and then was parted from them.[44] In John's Gospel we hear of an appearance to Mary Magdalene who at first failed to recognise Jesus, and when she did was forbidden to touch him;[45] this is followed by two appearances to the disciples in which Jesus appeared and disappeared without warning to and from a locked room;[46] finally John records an appearance to the disciples while fishing in which, once more, Jesus was not initially recognised.[47]

That Jesus' closest friends often failed to recognise him; that they were divided between adoration and scepticism; and that Jesus was able to appear and vanish at will, are features of the Gospel narratives which seem to support St Paul's view that the appearances of Jesus to the disciples were akin to his own experience of Jesus appearing 'within him'.[48]

I suggest therefore that the first theories we should test are those which assume the appearances to have been visionary experiences enjoyed by the first disciples. But what gave rise to these experiences? Bultmann suggests that 'the historian' might explain them as 'a series of subjective visions' brought about by 'the personal intimacy which the disciples had enjoyed with Jesus during his earthly life.'[49] But as Professor Wilckens says, before we could accept such an explanation 'we would have to demonstrate that such a thing was possible. And precisely because it is quite impossible that disciples of Jesus should have reacted to the catastrophe of his death by the conviction suddenly dawning upon them that he had been raised from the dead — which had never previously been asserted in Israel of any mortal — the so-called hypothesis of the subjective vision must be excluded as an explanation.'[50]

The point here is that subjective hallucinations require a sense of emotional expectancy and longing, and this condition was not fulfilled by the disciples and perhaps especially not St Paul. As Professor Lampe argues, 'Paul was persecuting the Christians because he thought that Jesus had been a false prophet or bogus Messiah. It is hard to think that his experience on the road to Damascus was a piece of unconscious self-deception or wish-fulfilment. And it seems clear from what took place after the arrest of Jesus, that Peter and the other disciples had not hoped that this would happen.' Lampe further argues that all the evidence about the disciples' state of mind indicates that the 'experience of encounter with the living Lord . . . came to them out of the blue when they were least expecting it.'[51]

In short the objection to the concept of a self-originating subjective vision is that such a vision could not provide an

adequate explanation for the dramatic psychological change
in the disciples' own minds, nor could it provide that
empowering sense of the presence of Christ with them. In the
final analysis a subjective vision is a form of vivid memory
and as Professor Lampe argues: 'However vivid the memory
of great men may be, even to the extent that we may wish to
speak of 'feeling their presence around us', we are surely
aware that we cannot use such language literally . . . The
disciples, I believe, knew themselves encountered by an
actual living presence, and this was the presence of the Lord,
who was none other than the Jesus whom they had known,
or, in the case of Paul, known of.'[52]

I think that Lampe's argument holds, and therefore urge
that the only vision theory adequate to account for the
disciples' faith is one which asserts that the visions were
objectively real. By this I mean that the source and
inspiration of the visions was external to the disciples and did
not originate in their own thinking, even though they would
naturally have been mediated through the subjective consciousness of each individual disciple. Professor Lampe makes
a strong defence of this position:

> If the appearances to the apostles were private mani-
> festations in the sense that a casual bystander would have
> seen nothing: if, that is to say, they were in the nature of
> visions rather than of bodily seeing, this does not imply
> that these men were not confronted with the Lord's
> presence as an external reality. To maintain the contrary
> would be to pass a very sweeping and damaging judgement
> on a great body of religious experience. It would be hard
> to think that because, in all probability, no other
> worshipper in the Temple saw anything remarkable when
> Isaiah 'saw the Lord, high and lifted up' (Isaiah 6/1 ff.),
> therefore the prophet dreamed up the experience and that
> the Lord's presence never impinged upon him as an
> objective reality. It does mean however, that, as this
> example from the Old Testament indicates, the Easter
> appearances were not dissimilar in kind from other
> phenomena in the history of religious experience.[53]

Lampe's analogical use of Isaiah's vision lends itself to the view described, but not held, by Archbishop Ramsey, that the visions were 'imparted by God himself, so as to assure the disciples that Jesus was alive and that his gracious activity was with them in a new and enhanced manner.'[54] In the words of Theodor Keim, the principal exponent of the theory, the visions served as 'a telegram from heaven' to provide the disciples with 'evidence that Jesus was alive.'[55] Such a hypothesis would fit many of the facts.

It would explain the revitalisation of the disciples and at the same time do justice to the ambiguity of their response. For like any religious experience some might respond to it, be transformed, encouraged and moved to worship, while others, completely unmoved, would be doubtful that the experience had any reality to it. Like all religious experience such divinely inspired visions would be mediated through the disciples' own thinking and hence would be dependent upon their receptivity, sensitivity, and religious background.

Such an hypothesis would fit particularly well the description Paul gives of his conversion experience in Galatians 1/16: 'God called me through his grace and chose to reveal his Son in me'. Furthermore the hypothesis has a clarity and simplicity about it which does much to commend it and I am particularly impressed by Lampe's point that it relates the Easter appearances of Jesus to other phenomena in the history of religious experience.[56] Thus I consider that the 'Telegram-from-Heaven' theory has a strong claim to be considered as a reasonable way of interpreting Christ's Easter appearances.

On the other hand there are weaknesses in the theory. Although it accords so well with Galatians 1/16, it clashes with the other five accounts we have of Paul's conversion experience in all of which the vision is directly attributed to Jesus himself.[57] The theory is also hard to square with other New Testament data. As B.H. Streeter pointed out: 'Although ... the men of that age were in the habit of taking visions very seriously as Divine messages ... they did very clearly distinguish between the appearances of the risen Lord and the ordinary visions which are so frequently mentioned in the New Testament and elsewhere; and considering the vital importance to them of the question, one ought at least to weigh gravely the probability that they had reasonable grounds for making the distinction.'[58]

Streeter suggests that we should consider instead the possibility that the visions were 'directly caused by the Lord himself veritably alive and personally in communion with them.'[59] On this view Jesus' conquest of death should be understood in terms of the immortality of his soul, or in Streeter's own phrase, his 'personal immortality'. His resurrection would then consist in the fact that he was able 'to convince the disciples of His victory over death by some adequate manifestation; possibly by showing Himself to them in some form such as might be covered by St Paul's phrase, "a spiritual body" or possibly through some psychological channel similar to that which explains the mystery means of communication between persons commonly known as telepathy'.[60]

Streeter's suggestion has been taken up by Archdeacon Michael Perry in his work *The Easter Enigma* in which he argues that the appearances of Jesus can be understood as veridical hallucinations, telepathically induced in the disciples' minds by Jesus' surviving soul.[61] The advantages of this theory can best be understood by considering some of the findings which have been made about such phenomena by the Society for Psychical Research.

In his Myer's Memorial Lecture for 1942, G.N.M. Tyrell analysed 1684 reports of 'Apparitions' gathered by this society. He stated that the apparitions seemed to the percipients to be as real as something objectively seen,[62] but that french chalk, cameras, and tape-recorders never provide evidence of an apparition's presence.[63] Apparitions sometimes appear in locked rooms, at times they vanish suddenly, at other times they fade away; they normally evade touching and they leave no physical traces of their presence behind them; they are seen by some, but not others of those present.[64] Many features of Jesus' resurrection appearances seem to fit this general pattern: he appears suddenly in a locked room,[65] he vanishes,[66] or is slowly 'parted from them';[67] he is seen by some and not others of those present;[68] he says at one time, 'touch me not.'[69] These features of Jesus' appearances seem to have much more in common with reports of apparitions than with accounts of objective seeings.

But what is an apparition? It is on this point that Tyrell's analysis seems most profound. His position is best summed up by Perry: 'The information on which the apparition is based comes from outside the percipient, but the form of the apparition is a creation of his own mind. His unconscious self dramatises this information in the form of a hallucination which appears to be external to the percipient'.[70] It is easy to see how ghost stories can be explained by this hypothesis: thus a person told of some appalling tragedy might be so moved in the silence of the night he might 'see' the pathetic victim in his imagination. Likewise, a man burdened by a guilty past like Brutus or Macbeth in Shakespeare's plays, might at a moment of crisis 'see' once more the person he had wronged.[71] There would have been nothing surprising if individual disciples of Jesus had been haunted by a vision of their suffering leader in his dying agony upon the cross. But brooding on such a tragedy could not begin to explain their joyful and triumphant vision of Christ overcoming death and rising to glorious life. The inspiration for this vision could not have come from knowledge of what had happened in the past as in a ghost story, but rather must have been based on new information vouchsafed to the disciples.

I argue therefore that the apparitions of Jesus should be likened not to ghost stories, but rather to the much more common accounts of apparitions of the living. In these cases the information on which the apparition is based seems to come from the person whose likeness is seen, to whom we can refer as the 'agent.' Archdeacon Perry writes, 'In the spontaneous cases the agent is generally undergoing some severe mental and physical shock, either of accident or death. It may be that one of the effects of this shock could be automatically to stimulate into exceptional activity whatever part of the agent is responsible for the initiation of an hallucination in the percipient.' There are many cases on the files of the S.P.R. when a percipient 'sees' an apparition of the agent at the precise moment when the agent is undergoing some traumatic experience.[72] 'This kind of hallucination is called "veridical". It is an hallucination because what is seen is physically not there; it is veridical because it is observed in connection with a real event outside the percipient's normal knowledge.'[73]

As well as these spontaneous cases there are also reports of experimental cases in which the agent caused an apparition of himself to be seen by willing it to happen. G.N.M. Tyrell claimed to have found sixteen cases where this experiment had been successful.[74] I suggest therefore that the apparitions of Jesus, seen by his disciples, can best be understood as veridical hallucinations, revealing truthfully the fact of Jesus' continued aliveness to the disciples' minds. I suggest that the source of this information was Jesus himself, communicating telepathically to his disciples.

This theory is supported by the consideration that telepathy is the only way a disembodied mind could communicate with an embodied one, and a veridical hallucination seems the only reasonable way to explain the clothed appearance of the risen Christ. Men never imagine Jesus manifesting himself naked to his disciples in the Upper Room, or to Cleopas and his companion on the road to Emmaus, or to Mary Magdalene in the garden. Unless one is prepared to postulate 'spiritual clothes' or 'the resurrection of Jesus' robe', one is in real difficulties in accounting for many of Jesus' appearances except by the hypothesis of hallucination. One could of course postulate readily available gardener's clothes for the incident in the garden, but not for those appearances which involved appearances and exits through locked doors.

This latter consideration of Jesus' clothes is one of the reasons why I find difficulty with what is perhaps the most natural way of accounting for the appearances, namely that Jesus appeared to his disciples in a spiritual body. Such a body would be subject to different laws from those which govern us at present and could therefore appear and disappear at will, and pass through locked doors. Such a doctrine of a spiritual body has the authority of St Paul to support it,[75] and has the added virtue that it makes it possible for one to combine belief in the empty tomb and bodily resurrection of Jesus with a full recognition of the oddities associated with Jesus' appearances. One could suppose with C.F.D. Moule that, 'The material of which the body (i.e. the corpse of Jesus) was composed was somehow transformed into a different mode of existence (such as practically all Christians believe characterised the Jesus of the Easter experience).'[76] Such a view would release Christian belief from such philosophically awkward concepts as 'disembodied souls, "telepathy", and veridical hallucinations.'

However I do not think the concept is valid, for I am impressed by Don Cupitt's argument that a 'spiritual body' is a logical hybrid. The body is considered tangible enough to be seen, yet intangible enough to pass through locked doors. It seems, as Don Cupitt suggests, to belong to those "theories which postulate a para-normal seeing of a para-normal object, which it is commonly claimed, is nevertheless available to historical investigation . . . [77] it has to be odd enough to overturn our world view and yet fall under rules of evidence which pre-suppose our normal world view.'[78] It has to be tangible enough to be seen and heard with the physical organs and strong enough to support clothes, and yet intangible enough to pass through the walls of the upper room. I therefore regard the notion of a physically visible spiritual body as an impossible compromise position between a resurrected corpse and a veridical hallucination.

So far my discussion of the nature of Jesus' resurrection has been based entirely on the accounts of Jesus' appearances to his disciples, and within these I have confined my attention to those elements which cohere with the theory of veridical hallucination. But the New Testament also contains material which cannot possibly accord with such a theory. There is the tradition of the empty tomb, and there are references to Jesus' risen body possessing 'flesh and bones',[79] 'eating and drinking' with his disciples,[80] and being sufficiently tangible for Thomas to be invited to touch him.[81] What are we to make of these traditions?

Many scholars believe that the story of the empty tomb is one of the foundation Christian beliefs. C.F.D. Moule quotes with approval the opinion that 'Whether or not we today can believe it in a literal sense, the tradition of the empty tomb is at any rate not a late accretion but is part of the earliest traditions.'[82] J.A. Baker states, 'The event may be unique, mysterious, supernatural; but every principle of historical argumentation demands that it be true.'[83]

In St Paul's account of the tradition that he had inherited he includes the comment that 'Jesus was raised on the third day, in accordance with the scriptures.' (1 Corinthians 15/4). It seems most unlikely that the Old Testament texts hinted at here (Hosea 6/2, or Jonah 1/17) would of themselves have given rise to such a belief, so Lillie argues that 'it is much more likely that the reappearance of Jesus on the third day was a historical fact and that later Christian preachers . . . sought for Old Testament texts with some correspondence to it'.[84] J.N.D. Anderson similarly points to the institution of Sunday and Easter in the Christian calendar as evidence that something startling happened on that third day.[85] Both Lillie and Anderson imply that only the discovery of the empty tomb would be a sufficient explanation, but I suggest that the first appearance of Jesus to his disciples would of itself set that third day apart as a momentous occasion.

A second argument for the empty tomb is drawn from the same text, this time concentrating on the word 'buried'. As Lillie expresses it, 'When St Paul wrote . . . that "Christ died . . . that he was buried [and] that he was raised on the third day",[86] he implies that just as it was a physical body that was crucified and buried, so it was a physical body that was raised.'[87] Both Ramsey and Moule find this argument convincing[88] but Lampe believes that the words do not necessarily imply a bodily resurrection, and 'since there is no mention of an empty tomb it probably does not.' Although argument from silence is usually dangerous, I believe Lampe is right to state that in the situation to which Paul was writing, 'the argument from silence has unusual force,' for he was writing to men who were denying that there was a resurrection and therefore needed every possible argument that could support his case. 'Had he known that the tomb was empty it seems inconceivable that he should not have adduced this here as a telling piece of objective evidence.'[89]

A third argument used to suggest that Paul believed in a physical resurrection cites the reaction given to his sermon at Athens when he preached on 'Jesus and the resurrection.'[90]

Lillie comments 'His preaching aroused a mockery that a sound Platonic doctrine of the immortality of the soul would never have caused.'[91] This seriously overstates the case, for although some mocked, others asked to hear Paul again, and a few were converted.[92] Moreover we are explicitly told that the audience consisted of Epicurean and Stoic philosophers[93] to whom the concept of immortality would have been just as unacceptable as that of resurrection. It was not till much later that most Stoics accepted an immaterial concept of the soul, while Epicureans were always opposed to any idea of a future life.[94] Moreover I suggest that Lillie unduly limits the alternatives open to St Paul through his implicit assumption that unless Paul taught the resuscitation of Jesus' corpse, then he must have taught a Platonic doctrine of immortality. It seems much more reasonable to assume that Paul put forward his own highly sophisticated understanding of the resurrection of Jesus, as expressed in 1 Corinthians 15. Here, while placing all his emphasis on resurrection, he states categorically that 'flesh and blood cannot inherit the kingdom of God.'[95] I support Lampe's view that this remark makes it 'difficult to think that Paul could possibly have believed that Jesus rose from the grave as, or in, a physical body.' Further, this comment indicates that Paul could not have known of the more corporeal elements in the resurrection stories. 'If the body of the risen Christ could be handled, and if he truly ate food, then . . . flesh and blood manifestly did inherit the kingdom of God.'[96]

It is of course possible that Paul thought that Jesus' corpse had been transformed from a body of flesh and blood into a spiritual body which did not exist spatially. But I agree with Lampe that the way Paul talks about grain and corn drying, and about the dissolution of our bodily frame, makes this improbable.[97] Hence I believe that the Easter tradition, as known to St Paul, did not include the Empty Tomb.

Turning to the Gospels, the situation changes. Scholars seem seriously divided about whether the Empty Tomb traditions within the Gospels are early or late, historical or fanciful. One school of thought supports J.B. Phillips' subjective analysis that the stories have the ring of truth about them.[98] Lillie comments that there is 'a restraint in the

Gospel narratives which give a *prima facie* appearance of historical reliability.'[99]

Lillie argues that the appearances of Christ to the woman (Matthew 28/9,10), to the eleven disciples (Matthew 28/16–20), and to the disciples (John 20/19–21) follow the common pattern of pronouncement stories. In less elaborate form, the pattern is also seen in the appearances to the eleven (Mark 16/14–15; Luke 24/36–49) to Mary Magdalene (John 20/11–17), and to Thomas (John 20/26–29). The significance of this is that 'In the opinion of many form critics, this is the type of narrative likely to have the greatest historical reliability, and there is no reason whatever (except our modern dread of the supernatural) to deny this historical reliability to the essential elements in the post-resurrection narratives.'[100]

The story of the road to Emmaus contains a full summary of the story of the Empty Tomb, and according to Martin Dibelius 'This story has been preserved in an almost pure form.' Lillie comments that if a story-teller had been constructing this tale, he would hardly have chosen such obscure heroes as a disciple not mentioned elsewhere and his un-named companion.[101]

C.F.D. Moule draws attention to the fact that the Empty Tomb narratives 'came to be framed almost exlusively of women witnesses, who as such were notoriously invalid witnesses according to Jewish principles of evidence. The later and more fictitious the story, the harder it is to explain why the Apostles are not brought to the forefront as witnesses.'[102] J.A. Baker agrees with this reasoning, saying 'That it should be these devoted but humble and relatively insignificant followers who are given the credit for the discovery in every Gospel is historically impressive.'[103]

Hence there is a substantial consensus of scholars who defend the historicity of the Empty Tomb. Archbishop Ramsey adds his testimony: 'To the Empty Tomb witness is borne by the narrative of Mark, by reference within the Emmaus story in Luke, and by the tradition in John. It is possible that John's story of Mary Magdalene goes back to a tradition as early as the tradition about the women recorded in St Mark. It is certain that we have the testimony of the earliest Gospel and of cross-reference in a Lucan tradition. Are traditions thus attested in the Gospels and congruous with the primitive preaching to be discredited, apart from *a priori* consideration?'[104]

These are powerful arguments from very distinguished scholars. On the other hand, no one claims that the Gospel stories are earlier than St Paul's testimony, and as I have argued, Paul does not seem to have known of the doctrine, and therefore it cannot have been part of the very earliest tradition. Further, I am impressed by Professor Lampe's argument that the stories of the Empty Tomb 'have, like the infancy narratives, the characteristics of myth. Angels, visible in human form, appear as characters in the narrative and address the chief actors; an angel descends from heaven, rolls away the stone which sealed the rock tomb and sits upon it.'[105]

Such mythical elements seem to point to a period of reflection and militate against the idea that we are dealing with a primitive tradition. However, the fatal objection to the narratives is their internal incoherence. I do not mean by this the problem of whether the appearances were in Galilee or Jerusalem; nor do I refer to minor inconsistencies like the difference of opinion as to how many women went into the tomb,[106] or whether the witness at the tomb was one or two young men or one, two, or a whole vision of angels.[107] The internal incoherence of which I speak concerns the nature of the body of Jesus. Even the most corporeal accounts in Luke and John refer to Jesus suddenly appearing from nowhere into the middle of a room.[108] A body which can do this is not a resuscitated corpse. In order to account for the body passing through the doors we should have to suppose that it de-materialised outside the doors and was then re-constituted inside; but how would such a reconstitution differ from a re-creation *ex nihilo*? If we suppose that the dead body of Jesus de-materialised, then, as matter, it ceased to exist, and there would be no material continuity between the body laid in the tomb, and the body eating fish with the disciples.[109]

Moreover if Jesus' corpse had been transformed into a spiritual body, what was it doing eating fish? If Jesus did not need to eat, then this smacks of a supernatural conjuring trick of the kind he abjured during his life.[110]    But if he needed food then his body was not spiritual. Similarly if his body were capable of being touched, it would ipso facto be incapable of passing through locked doors, unless we suppose it was constantly changing its nature, but the notion of Jesus' clothing keeping in step with such changes seems to me to rule out this as a credible hypothesis.

Hence I conclude that the traditions which imply that Jesus' corpse was raised from the grave should be rejected as internally incoherent. My conviction that Jesus really appeared to his disciples is therefore necessarily associated with the theory of Jesus' soul being his true self, continuing to exist after the death of his body, and manifesting his presence to the disciples through a telepathic communication to their minds.

I am of course conscious that this is not the way any of the first Christians described the situation, but I think this was because they did not have the concept of telepathic veridical hallucination at their disposal. They described their experience in the thought-forms of their day, and resurrection was the concept most suitable for expressing the conviction of the reality of Jesus' presence to them. Once the word had been used, then a progressively corporeal understanding of the concept was a natural development.

However, it has been suggested that the very use of the word 'resurrection' implies a physical resuscitation. According to Dr Jacques Choron, 'resurrection of the dead' literally meant 'uprising of the corpses.'[111] Lillie believes that 'To Jews of the first century resurrection almost certainly meant physical resurrection. The disciples would think of rising again in the fashion of Ezekiel 37 with its reference to sinews, flesh, skin and breath, rather than in Greek fashion of an immortal soul escaping from an imprisoning body.'[112]

This assertion is based on the presupposition that Jews of the first century shared the same understanding of what it means to be a person as their ancestors centuries before them, and it assumes that in the context of first century Judaism it is still possible to draw a sharp distinction between 'Hebrew' and 'Greek' thought.

I suggest that a better method of approach will avoid

laying down in advance what a Jew of the first century must have thought, and will consider what he actually did think. I believe that there is ample evidence to show that at that time Hebrew religious thinkers were as pluralistic in their thinking about life after death as any contemporary national grouping.

The New Testament tells us that the Sadducees believe 'that there is no resurrection, nor angel, nor spirit.'[113] Josephus writes that the Essenes 'taught the same doctrine as the sons of Greece' about the immortality of the soul,[114] while according to Professor G.R. Driver, the Covenanters of Qumran 'had some vague notions of physical resurrection, and certainly believed in a future angelic existence with God . . . but perhaps not in any resurrection of the body.'[115] By contrast however, it seems likely that the Pharisees believed that the dead would rise again at the last day.[116] Hence, in the four first century Jewish groups best known to us, we see represented exactly the same range of views as one might find among Christian groups today: belief in extinction at death, or in the immortality of the soul, or in resurrection but not of this present body, or in corporeal resuscitation at the end of time. Indeed, not even these four possibilities are exhaustive, for according to Choron, 'Even transmigration found its way into Judaism . . . It appears in the "Cabala"; [and] is found systematised in the "Zohar".'[117] Moreover, C.F.D. Moule says that belief that man could survive death 'in an immaterial spectre-like form' was 'well-attested among Jews.'[118]

In fact, as in any pluralist society, the Jews of the first century were thoroughly confused in their own minds about what to believe. Professor C.F. Evans shows that the Qumran scrolls show a wide variety of beliefs within one sect,[119] and D.S. Russell shows that Jewish Apocalyptic writers working within a common religious framework 'reveal a bewildering variation of opinion over the future state.'[120]

The popular distinction between 'Greek' and 'Hebrew' thinking on this matter is a most unhelpful categorisation for beliefs held about the after-life in the first century. It is generally recognised that R.H. Charles 'was unequalled in his understanding of the entire body of Jewish apocalyptic literature available during his life-time',[121] and he was quite

categorical in his judgement that 'it was not necessary for
Israel to borrow from Greece the idea that the soul could
preserve its powers independently of the body.'[122] Tensions
within Jewish thought alone gave rise 'gradually to the
apprehension that man's soul is capable of divine life beyond
the grave.'[123] D.S. Russell, the outstanding contemporary
authority on 'The Method and Message of Jewish Apocalyptic', reports that in the extra-biblical writings we can discern
'a radical change in men's beliefs concerning the nature of
survival in the life after death . . . Previously, in Old Testament thought, personality was wholly dependent on body
for its expression; now it could be expressed — in some
limited way at least — in terms of discarnate soul, which,
though possessing form and recognisable appearance, could
live in separation from the body which had been left behind
at death.'[124] Professor James Barr writes 'It is quite easy to
show that in late Judaism the soul could be regarded as
separate from the body. This may, indeed, be explained as a
result of Hellenistic influence. It may also however, and
perhaps better, be taken as in principle the result of tensions
and problems within Judaism itself.'[125]

If we look at the New Testament without the a priori
supposition that all first century Jews must have believed in
the physical resuscitation of our corpses, we find considerable evidence pointing to a much more spiritual understanding of a future life than the New Testament has been
given credit for. In the only categorical statement Jesus is
reported to have made about the resurrection state, he
described the pharisaic position as 'quite wrong'[126] and
described resurrection life in terms of being 'like angels in
heaven.'[127]

St Paul explicitly denies that 'flesh and blood can inherit
the kingdom of God',[128] and in 2 Corinthians 5/6—8 writes
that 'as long as we are in the body we are exiles from the
Lord . . . We would rather leave our home in the body and go
to live with the Lord.' This language seems quite explicitly to
identify the person with the soul, and once we grasp that a
first century Jew could quite easily have made such an
identification, there seems no valid reason for supposing that
Paul did not mean what he says here. It seems quite

reasonable to think that St Paul understood Jesus' resurrection in terms of an existence closer akin to angelic existence than to our present life. This would fit well with the tremendous contrast Paul draws between earthly and spiritual existence in 1 Corinthians 15. Hence I suggest that St Paul believed that Jesus rose from the dead into a spiritual existence without supposing that anything unusual happened to Jesus' corpse.

I suggest that Paul used the word 'resurrection' to indicate that it was Jesus' total person which had conquered death — not just his intellectual life, but his whole personaltity. Hence I agree with Bishop Montefiore's description of resurrection as 'the resurrection of human personality' of which 'Jesus is the first fruits.'[129] And this, I believe, is what Paul was trying to communicate. I think this because St Paul regarded it as axiomatic that Christ's resurrection is the primary grounds for supposing that we too may live beyond the grave,[130] and hence we are false to Paul's most basic belief if we interpret the resurrection of Jesus in such a way as to make it radically different from what we may expect to be our own destiny.

As Professor Lampe argues, to believe

> that Christ's resurrection is the assurance that we too shall rise from the dead implies that his resurrection was not different in kind from what we may hope for through him. Yet if his body was raised physically from the grave and did not see corruption, or if his body was transformed after death into something different in such a way that it was annihilated then . . . his entry into life beyond the grave was different from what we hope may be our own.[131]

But if we interpret Jesus' resurrection as the triumph of his 'personality' or 'soul' over the death of his body, then it can become a basis for us to hope that we too may live anew after the dissolution of our bodies. This argument seems expressed in the First Epistle of Peter where we read that 'after the death of his body he [Jesus] came alive in the spirit', and consequently the dead have hope that, 'although in the body they have received the sentence common to men, they might in the spirit be alive with the life of God'.[132]

St Paul expresses a similar conviction, 'He who raised the Lord Jesus to life will raise us too . . . for we know that if the earthly frame that houses us today should be demolished we possess a building which God has provided . . . eternal and in heaven.'[133]

However this way of interpreting the data is not at all common among New Testament scholars. Professor Wolfhart Pannenberg, for example, takes a very different line in his influential book *Jesus, God and Man.*[134] Pannenberg insists that Christian belief cannot dispense with the apocalyptic framework in which so much of the New Testament teaching is set: 'The basis on which the understanding of Jesus rests is always linked to the apocalyptic framework of Jeṣus' earthly life . . . if this framework is removed, then the fundamental basis of faith is lost.'[135] Pannenberg points out that according to St Paul our resurrection will take place not when we die, but at the end of time;[136] Christ was raised first 'and afterwards, at his coming, those who belong to Christ. Then comes the end when he delivers up the kingdom of God at the last trumpet call.'[137] Pannenberg argues that Christ is the first fruits of the dead, in that what happened to him will happen to us at the end of time; in Jesus the final resurrection of the last day was anticipated to confirm his authority, and to reveal to us the final divine eschatological plan, in the light of which we must revise our understanding of history, and our expectation of future life.[138]

The great difficulty of Pannenberg's position is that the whole notion of a general resurrection at the last day seems so bizarre in the light of what we know of the universe, and the framework of our thinking about life and history. As Pannenberg himself says, 'universal resurrection of the dead is not imaginable within this present world.'[139] But I do not find that the concept grows any easier to imagine simply by projecting it to the end of time, and in subsequent chapters I shall spell out just how immense the difficulties are in thinking in these terms today.

There is no doubt that there are two diverse traditions in the New Testament evidence relating to Jesus' resurrection, and that scholars are deeply divided as to how this data is to be interpreted. I have tried to indicate the grounds on which

I have concluded that the data can most reasonably be interpreted in terms of Jesus' surviving soul communicating his continued aliveness to the disciples by telepathically induced veridical hallucinations. But in expounding both my own and other writers' views, I am conscious that there is a very intimate relationship between a man's interpretation of the New Testament evidence and what he believes to be essential to personal identity, and necessary for personal existence beyond the grave. Thus Professor Lampe rejects a physical interpretation of Jesus' resurrection at least partly because he believes that it is quite impossible for a modern Christian to expect his corpse to be raised to new life, either at the moment of death or at the end of time.[140] On the other hand Professor Pannenberg puts his stress on the empty tomb,[141] and insists that we must rehabilitate the apocalyptic framework of the first century and expect a universal resurrection of the dead at the end of time. And Pannenberg believes this to be necessary . . . at least partly because he holds that the concept of the undying continuation of the soul while the body perishes has become untenable today.[142]

Hence the way in which one interprets what the New Testament says about the nature of Jesus' resurrection depends, to a great extent, on the conclusions one comes to on other grounds about the likelihood of a bodily resurrection, and the validity of the concept of the soul. Inquiry into these themes will occupy most of the rest of this book.

# Part II

# 3 The Traditional Belief in the Resurrection of the Flesh

Traditional Christian belief has understood Jesus' resurrection in a quite straightforward way. As the fourth article of the Church of England puts it: 'Christ did truly rise again from death, and took again his body, with flesh, bones, and all things pertaining to the perfection of Man's nature; wherewith he ascended into heaven, and there sitteth.' The significance of this for us was thought to be equally clear. What happened to Jesus then will happen to us at the end of time. The 'particles composing each individual's flesh' will be collected together,[1] the 'sea will give up its dead',[2] the cannibal will restore the flesh he has borrowed,[3] and 'the identical structure which death had previously destroyed' will be restored.[4] This doctrine of the 'Resurrection of the Flesh' was incorporated in the Apostles' Creed; it was declared *de fide* for the Roman Catholic by the Fourth Lateran Council; it was the traditional teaching of the Church of England as shown by the Book of Homilies and by Hooker; it was taught in Calvin's Institutes, and in Luther's small Catechism.[5] As such it has a good claim to be regarded as part of the basic faith of western Christendom throughout the ages. But is it a credible belief today? To answer that question let us consider why the Christian Fathers came to believe in and to defend this doctrine, and see how far their arguments hold good today.

The main reason why most of the Christian Fathers insisted on the Resurrection of the Flesh was their belief that only bodily continuity could ensure personal survival. Although they believed in the immortality of the soul, they felt that this on its own was insufficient.[6] Irenaeus argued that

'Spirit with the flesh taken away would not be a spiritual man, but the spirit of a man.'[7] According to Athenagoras, 'Man is soul and body, one harmony and community of experience belonging to the whole being.'[8] Centuries later Aquinas summed up this line of argument in his famous statement 'My soul is not I, and if only souls are saved, *I* am not saved, nor is any man.'[9] This is precisely what the Fathers had taught. 'Is the Lost Sheep to be saved without his body?' asked Tertullian;[10] 'The reality of resurrection without flesh and bones, without blood and members is unintelligible;' asserted Jerome.[11]

Time has done nothing to weaken the force of this argument. If personal identity depends on bodily continuity, then I will only live again if my corpse is raised from the grave. But is the Patristic expectation of such raising a reasonable hope for us to share? They defended their belief by appealing to the requirements of justice, to analogies from nature, and to Biblical testimony. Let us examine their case.

Athenagoras argues that without fleshly resurrection men would not get their deserts, 'since many . . . persons who practice every . . . wickedness live on to the last, unvisited by calamity, whilst others who lived an exemplary life live in pain'.[12] Justice demands recompense in a future life. But if such recompense were paid to the soul alone this would be completely unjust. 'If good deeds are rewarded the body will be wronged if it is not rewarded, inasmuch as it shared in the toils connected with well doing', while if faults are to be punished, it would be unjust for the soul to be punished for sins of the flesh 'for which its own nature feels no appetite'.[13] Justice therefore demands, as Tertullian says, that 'man must be judged as a whole'.[14] Rufinus urges that through the resurrection of 'this flesh', 'it becomes possible in recompense for the struggles of the present life, for the flesh to be crowned along with its soul, and for the immoral flesh to be punished.'[15] John of Damascus writes, 'Since the soul does not pursue either vice or virtue separate from the body, both together will obtain that which is their just due.'[16]

If we grant their premises, then the Fathers' conclusions follow. If in the end all virtue must be fairly rewarded and all vice justly punished, and if bodily continuity is necessary for the identity of the moral agent to remain constant, then it does indeed follow that corpses must be restored to life for justice to be meted out to men. But is the notion of retributive justice valid? Do we still believe that a moral order requires that there be a balance between punishment and sin? I suggest that such ideas find few defenders today. To most of us, punishment seems better defended as a means to reform the offender or as a deterrent. Punishment is seen as a regrettable necessity, not a good cancelling out an evil to restore a moral balance in the universe. Hence I believe that the notion of raising a man from the dead simply that he might be punished for the evil he committed during his life seems an obnoxious doctrine to most people today; especially since eternal punishment must of necessity be infinitely out of proportion to any conceivable crime. I suggest therefore that the argument from retributive justice which seemed so convincing to the early Fathers carries little conviction to twentieth century thinkers.

Let us turn therefore to the second patristic defence of the rationality of fleshly resurrection — the arguments drawn from analogies with nature. Tertullian for example defends the resurrection hope by appealing to the much greater wonder of the original creation:

'All agree either that God created the Universe out of nothing, or that he moulded it from underlying matter.' Therefore God must be able to re-make it for 'You must believe that the restoration of flesh is easier than its creation.'[17] Pseudo-Justin argues in the same vein that just as 'Sculptors and painters renew their works when they fall into decay', so too God, the supreme artist, is able to renew his creations when they decay.[18]

Irenaeus develops this argument with reference to the creation of the first man: 'It was much more difficult and incredible — from non-existent bones, and nerves, and veins and the rest of man's organisation — to make man an animated and rational creature, than to re-integrate that which had been created and after decomposed.'[19] Athenagoras argues that: 'The resurrection would only be impossible if God either did not know what was to be done or had no power to do it . . . But it is not possible for God to be ignorant either of the nature of the bodies to be raised as regards both the members entire and the particles of which they consist, or whether each of the dissolved particles pass.'[20]

From the standpoint of their own day all these arguments are sound. Given belief in a once-for-all act of creation on the pattern of Genesis 1, then the act of resurrection cannot be difficult for the all-powerful God. Given that God made the first man by direct action, the restoration of a decomposed man becomes an easy task. Given that man consists of particles, it is easy to believe that omnipotence could reassemble these particles. But today each of these premises has lost its validity, and hence the conclusions drawn from them cannot stand. That man as a species is a part of a slowly evolving process of life and in every respect continuous with the processes of nature from which he has emerged does not provide a congenial background for the idea of resurrection. Further, our increasing knowledge of the incredible complexity and constant changing of our physical components makes it difficult to see the resurrection as simply involving the re-collection of our physical particles. We are not composed of building bricks but of constantly changing living matter.

A second analogy for resurrection seemed available to the Fathers in contemplating the mystery of the original development of each man in his mother's womb, or from his father's sperm. Irenaeus uses the mystery of our development in the womb.[21] Pseudo-Justin, Cyril, and Athenagoras appeal to our growth from sperm.[22] Athenagoras presents the case best: 'Would any believe unless taught by experience that in the soft seed alike in all its parts there was deposited such a variety and number of great powers, or of masses, which in this way arise and become consolidated — I mean of bones and nerves and cartilages, of muscles too and flesh and intestines and the other parts of the body. For neither in the moist seed anything of the kind is seen nor in infants do any of those things make their appearance which pertain to adults.' Athenagoras goes on to argue 'though neither the seed has inscribed upon it the life and form of man, nor the life and dissolution into primary elements, yet the succession of natural occurrences makes things credible which have no credibility apart from the phenomena themselves.'[23]

In other words to Athenagoras future resurrection seemed no more unlikely than our development from formless seed in our present life. But today this argument does not hold. We now know that the seed does have 'inscribed upon it the life and form of the man'; we call this inscription our DNA code.[24] Our development is not a total mystery for to a limited extent we can describe how it happens. What we now know of the development of the human embryo so far from providing an analogy for resurrection in fact militates against such a belief, for modern knowledge has made it so clear to us that our development as an embryo lies very firmly within the natural order and requires no special divine intervention.

The same criticism must be levelled against attempts by the Fathers to prove that 'All nature suggests resurrection' (Minucius Felix).[25] The argument is also used by Tertullian and Tatian.[26] Flowers die, decompose and rot, yet next year rise up from the dead. Stars die, yet re-emerge to view; each month the moon wanes, yet rises again, each day the sun sets in death to emerge victorious again on the morrow as *sol invicta*; each spring shrubs and trees get back their leaves, and the grass grows up once more. 'Nature teaches us to expect resurrection,' writes Tertullian 'for all nature was made for man': 'If all things rise again for man for whom they have been arranged, it follows that this cannot be for man unless for flesh also and therefore it is absurd to conclude that the thing itself should perish entirely, on whose account and for whom nothing perishes.'[27]

After death 'We must wait for springtime in the body'.[28] One inherent difficulty of this analogy was brought out centuries ago in the gentle irony of a Nisibene hymn, 'I marvel at this seed that after five thousand years its spring has not yet come.'[29] Modern knowledge concerning the germination of seeds in the ground has weakened the analogy still further, while the divorce of modern man from the seasons of the countryside has weakened even the poetic appeal of such images.

One final argument from nature must be mentioned – the

resurrection of the phoenix — quoted by Tertullian, I Clement, Cyril, Ambrose and the Apostolic Constitutions.[30] Tertullian regards this as conclusive evidence: the phoenix is a 'sufficient and undeniable example of this [resurrection] hope, for it is a breathing thing subject to death.' Psalm 92/11,[31] in his translation, promised 'Thou shalt flourish as does the phoenix'; so Tertullian argues that since the Lord declared that 'we are better than many sparrows' we can surely also assume that we are better than phoenixes; 'Shall men perish once for all while Arabian birds are sure of rising again?[32] Once more we hear an argument valid in the light of the knowledge of its own day but worthless in terms of modern natural history and indeed in terms of modern biblical translation which makes Tertullian's phoenix into a palm tree![33]

Thus for the Fathers in the Western tradition the resurrection of the flesh was morally necessary in the light of their understanding of justice; it was a reasonable belief if one considered their doctrine of Creation, their belief in the creation of the first man, their understanding of the development of the human embryo, their understanding of the order of nature, and on what they believed to be well founded observation of the habits of the phoenix. All these arguments enabled them to regard the Biblical teaching on the resurrection as reasonable within their total world view. Hence I do not accept Professor Wolfson's suggestion that fleshly resurrection was as much in conflict with ancient as with modern scientific knowledge.[34] On the contrary I think the examples I have given show just how much the patristic faith was buttressed by analogies based on a faulty understanding of the natural order.

But it is not only the Fathers' arguments from nature which have been weakened by modern knowledge, for if we examine their use of the Bible in the light of modern critical scholarship we find that Biblical evidence for the resurrection of the flesh is very much weaker than they had thought. A.M. Ramsey even going so far as to describe the doctrine as 'unscriptural.'[35]

The Fathers supposed that the doctrine of fleshly resurrection was taught throughout the Bible. 1 Clement quotes

Job 19/25 as saying 'Thou shalt raise up this flesh of mine which has suffered all these things.'[36] The exact meaning of this particular verse is notoriously difficult to determine and in the Septuagint, the Vulgate and the Authorised Version, the verse appears to teach that our flesh will be raised. However the consensus of modern scholarship inclines to the view that this is not its true meaning, but rather that Job hopes to be vindicated while he is still alive.

The most often quoted instance of apparent resurrection is Ezekiel's vision of the valley of dry bones.[37] At least nine of the Fathers looked on this episode as a historical event and deduced from it the conclusion that since large scale resurrection had taken place in the past, it could be reasonably expected to happen again in the future on an even larger scale.[38] Origen seems to have stood alone in teaching that the passage expresses in poetic imagery the future restoration of Israel.[39] Methodius disputed this argument on the grounds that the passage cannot refer to the restoration of the Jewish people from Babylon because, he alleges, this did not happen.[40] However modern scholarship seems to support Origen's judgement on this historical point, and it is now generally accepted that the vision must be taken figuratively.[41]

Tertullian and Irenaeus interpret Isaiah 40/5 as foretelling resurrection! 'All flesh shall see God's salvation.'[42] But like Ezekiel's dry bones this is now understood as a prophecy of Israel's restoration from exile, without any resurrection implications.[43]

Irenaeus interprets Isaac's blessing of Jacob and the promises of material abundance made to Israel by Isaiah, Ezekiel, and Daniel as all pointing to the glories of a future state.[44] But again modern scholarship rejects such interpretation as a total misapplication of the texts to a subject with which they were not concerned.[45]

To this misuse of the biblical material we must also add the Fathers' tendency to draw conclusions from fundamentalist use of the scriptural record and to build too much on obscure passages. Thus Irenaeus, Cyprian, the Apostolic Constitutions and Methodius all quote Enoch's translation as evidence for our bodily resurrection.[46] This obscure reference from the shadowy legends of Israel's beginnings could not be treated by contemporary Biblical critics as capable of sustaining the weight thus placed upon it. The same can be said of the ascension of Elijah as quoted by Irenaeus, Methodius and the Apostolic Constitutions,[47] or the three children in the burning fiery furnace cited by Tertullian and Irenaeus,[48] or Jonah cited by Irenaeus and the Apostolic Constitutions,[49] or the raising of the widow's son by Elijah and the Shunamite's son by Elisha, as quoted in the Constitutions.[50] All these quotations depend upon treating legendary, mythical or allegorical stories as if they were sober history. This is not really an open possibility for a modern person who reads his Bible with his understanding shaped by the insights of Biblical scholarship. If after careful investigation one comes to the conclusion that the story of Jonah was intended as an allegory of Israel's being swallowed up by Babylon and then vomited forth with a mission to other nations (cf. Jeremiah 51/34 and 51/44) it ceases to be possible to regard the story as a demonstration that men can be resurrected from the bodies of fish.[51] If one believes that Daniel is almost entirely legendary, written to encourage Maccabeans in their revolt, then one cannot regard the immunity to fire of the three children as evidence that, in a resurrection life, God's power can set this very flesh free from suffering.[52] One must conclude therefore that whereas the Fathers on their understanding of the Bible could find many quotations from the Old Testament to support their belief in fleshly resurrection, to a modern Biblical scholar the Old Testament support for such a doctrine is limited to Isaiah 26 quoted by Tertullian and Irenaeus and Augustine,[53] and Daniel 12 quoted by the Apostolic Constitutions.[54] These are two late and untypical passages and go against the main trend of Old Testament thought as described in Chapter 1.

Isaiah 26/19 states 'Thy dead shall live, their bodies shall rise. O dwellers in the dust awake and sing for joy!' Daniel 12/2 states: 'And many of those who sleep in the dust shall awake, some to everlasting life, and some to shame and everlasting contempt.' These texts almost certainly support the Fathers' use of them as evidence for resurrection of the flesh, for the references to graves and dust indicate a corporeal resurrection of a physical kind. But whereas for the Fathers these quotations were typical of the Old Testament teaching as a whole, for us they are two isolated quotations.

When we turn to the New Testament we find again that the Fathers appeal to a wide range of evidence which they interpret as pointing to a resurrection of the flesh, whereas modern scholarship insists that much of this evidence cannot bear the interpretation they give to it. Irenaeus and Tertullian cite 1 Thessalonians 5/23: 'Now may the God of peace sanctify you perfect, and may your spirit and soul and body be preserved whole without complaint to the coming of our Lord Jesus Christ.'[55] Irenaeus comments 'This prayer only has a purpose if St Paul was aware of the future re-integration and union of all three.' However today this passage is understood to refer to St Paul's expectation that the second coming would come in the lifetime of his readers.[56] A second quotation is Romans 8/11: 'But if the Spirit of him who raised up Jesus from the dead shall dwell in you, he that raised up Christ shall also quicken your mortal bodies.' 'What are mortal bodies?' asks Irenaeus ironically; 'Can they be souls?'[57] Here again Irenaeus seems to distort the sense of the original, for St Paul is not referring to physical resurrection but rather to moral reformation. If Irenaeus had not omitted the previous verse, St Paul's meaning would have been quite clear: 'But if Christ is dwelling within you, then although the body is a dead thing because you sinned, yet the spirit is life itself because you have been justified.'

A further New Testament quotation of doubtful relevance is 1 Corinthians 3/16: 'You are the Temple of God.' Irenaeus, following 2 Clement, argues that it is blasphemy to argue that the Temple of God in which the spirit dwells does not partake of salvation but is reduced to perdition.[58] One can reply to this as Jeremiah did to those who claimed the indestructibility of the Temple at Jerusalem: 'Go now to my place that was in Shiloh, where I first made my name to dwell, and see what I did to it.'[59]

The Latin Fathers get into great difficulties when faced with quotations which indicate that a future life will be very different from the present. 'Flesh and blood cannot inherit the kingdom of God'[60] and 'You shall be like the angels of heaven.'[61] Irenaeus tries to evade the first by arguing that 'flesh and blood does not inherit, but is inherited by, the spirit and translated to the kingdom of heaven.'[62] But he clearly found this approach unconvincing, for he later launches a frontal attack on the quotation: 'In every epistle the Apostle plainly states that through the flesh of our Lord and through his blood, we have been saved. If therefore flesh and blood are the things which procure life for us; it has not been declared that flesh and blood in the literal meaning cannot inherit the kingdom.'[63] Tertullian is more subtle. He suggests the inclusion of the word 'alone': 'Flesh and blood alone cannot inherit the kingdom of heaven. Spirit is also necessary.'[64] Tertullian further argues: 'A literal interpretation of flesh and blood would exclude Jesus from Heaven since Jesus still sits there at the right hand of the Father. He ascended in the same form also to descend'[65] (Acts 7/56; Mark 16/19). This shifts the ground and makes the argument over flesh and blood depend upon which interpretation one gives to Christ's own resurrection and ascension. If one supposes with the 4th Anglican article that Christ ascended into heaven with 'flesh, bones and all things appertaining to the perfection of man's nature', then Tertullian's argument is valid. If, however, one agrees with the Archbishop of Canterbury's Commission on Doctrine that 'the physical features [of the ascension narratives] are to be interpreted symbolically',[66] then Tertullian's argument loses all its force.

Pseudo-Justin, Jerome and Methodius try to explain away the reference to being like angels by suggesting that it refers to their way of life, rather than to their state.[67] Men will be like angels in behaviour and, though differences in sex will still persist, sexual intercourse will cease. The behaviour of holy virgins in this life indicates that possession of sexual organs does not necessarily lead to their use when a person dedicates himself to God. I find this interpretation wholly unconvincing, particularly since the Qumran Scrolls reveal that the expression 'As angels' was in common use in Jesus' day to indicate a spiritualised understanding of what resurrection meant.[68]

So far I have suggested that most of the New Testament

quotations used by the Fathers to justify belief in resurrection of the flesh are misapplied, and that their attempts to explain away the two most awkward texts against their view are unsatisfactory. Some of their further arguments depend upon a fundamentalist approach to the scriptures, such as arguments based on belief in a physical ascension of Jesus or on the historicity of accounts concerning the raising to life of Jairus' daughter, of Lazarus, and of the widow of Nain's son.[69] The same can be said against the arguments of the Apostolic Constitutions which depend on taking all the miracles of Christ as factual history.[70] The force of these arguments is weakened by the doubt in the minds of many contemporary critics about the likely historicity of these miracles. If for example the raising of Lazarus in John is a working out as history of what appears as a parable in Luke then its evidential value as an argument for physical resurrection is diminished.[71]

We now turn to the most important argument for the resurrection of the flesh, put foward by almost all the Fathers; namely that Jesus rose from the dead in the flesh and his resurrection is the first fruits of our resurrection. This argument forms the principal ground for expectation of our fleshly resurrection in the writings of Polycarp, Ignatius, Justin, Irenaeus, Tertullian, the Apostolic Constitutions, Cyprian, Eusebius, Pamphilius, Augustine, Rufinus and Jerome.[72] They discuss many of the New Testament texts which we considered in the previous chapter. The Fathers have no doubt that these texts refer explicitly to a resurrection in the flesh by Jesus, and to our subsequent fleshly resurrection in the same manner. But as we have already seen, the New Testament evidence is much more ambiguous than these Fathers supposed, and the consensus of modern biblical inquiry is that the New Testament evidence does not encourage belief in the future resuscitation of our corpses, nor that we should interpret the resurrection of Jesus as a literal resuscitation.

Thus we see that modern thinking in the field of moral philosophy, modern knowledge of evolution, DNA and natural history and modern understanding of the biblical data all undermine the arguments used by the Fathers in support of fleshly resurrection.

Moreover modern cosmological knowledge seems to make it impossible to continue to believe in both the resurrection of the flesh and a future eternal destiny in Heaven or Hell — one or other of the beliefs must go. But the Fathers are unanimous in supposing that Heaven constitutes the ultimate Christian hope, and in seeing our resurrection on earth as a purely temporary stage; whether this lasts only for a moment or for as long as a thousand years it is still only preparatory to endless bliss in heaven or endless woe in hell. Even those writers most preoccupied with thoughts of the millenium assert this.[73] Consequently, I suggest, belief in fleshly resurrection would suffer a fatal blow if it could be shown to be incompatible with belief in subsequent heavenly bliss. The Fathers experienced considerable tension in holding the two beliefs together. I suggest that modern knowledge has so increased this tension that the link must now snap.

The Christian Fathers seem to have accepted the same cosmological picture as that contained in the New Testament. 'The world is viewed as a three-storied structure, with the earth in the centre, the heaven above, and the underworld beneath. Heaven is the abode of God and celestial beings — the angels. The underworld is hell, the place of torment' (Rudolf Bultmann).[74] Dr Alan Richardson disputes this: 'In the Bible heaven and hell are not places, geographically identifiable; they are pictorial representations of nearness to God ... or of distance from God.'[75] He writes of Jesus' ascension thus, 'We have little idea of what in fact were St Luke's cosmological notions, but we may be sure that ... he is not telling us about the ascent of a physical body to a place above the sky. Heaven is not a place for the biblical writers.'[76]

Richardson is right to point out that occasionally the Bible uses the language of heaven figuratively, but on this central point he must be wrong because his argument could not be expressed in Hebrew, Greek, or Latin, or even in modern German or French.[77] The English language is unusual in that since the 17th Century the words 'sky' and 'heaven' have drifted apart in meaning;[78] consequently it is easy for an Englishman to forget that in ancient thought, and in most

other languages today, there is only one word for both
heaven and sky.

Hence when Luke tells us that Jesus went up into heaven[79]
he is also telling us that he went up into the sky, because
*ouranos* means both[80] and for any person in the ancient
world the two meanings would have been indistinguishable.

The Shorter Oxford English Dictionary gives the following
meanings to the word 'heaven': 'The realm or region of space
beyond the clouds of which the sky is viewed poetically as
the floor; the regions of space in which the heavenly bodies
move; each of the 'spheres' or spherical shells into which the
realm of space outside the earth were formally divided, the
number of which varied from 7–11; the celestial abode of
God and his angels, and of beautified spirits; the state of the
blessed hereafter.' Although this merely records the 'official'
English usage, these meanings do reflect what the word
'heaven' meant to the Christian Fathers, except that some
may have followed the Hebrew teaching that the floor of the
sky was as solid as anything could be,[81] and all would have
talked of the 'place' where the blessed would live hereafter,
rather than the 'state'.[82] Hence when the Fathers talked of
our going to heaven they were not using poetic images about
a future relationship with God, rather they were making
statements about the location to which they supposed our
resurrected and transformed bodies would ascend.

This can be seen rather vividly from the chapters St
Augustine devotes to 'the earthly bodies which the philosophers hold cannot be in heaven but must fall to earth by
their natural weight.'[83] and 'the platonists that oppose the
elevation of the body up to heaven, by arguments of
elementary ponderosity.'[84] Augustine's concern is to show
the reasonableness of supposing that resurrected earthly
bodies can physically ascend to a quite literal abode in the
sky. The main obstacle Augustine sees to resurrected bodies
living in the sky is their weight, so he tries to show how this
difficulty can be overcome. He points out that although lead
and iron are too heavy to float on water, man's skill 'can yet
frame a vessel that can swim', and if man can do this to iron
and lead surely God can do the same to our bodies![85] Then
what about birds? 'Why are there so many earthly bodies in

the air? . . . Cannot he that gave birds . . . feathers of power to sustain them in the air, give the like power to glorified and immortal bodies, to possess the heaven?'[86] Moreover 'if the angels can transport bodily weight whither they please . . . why may we not believe that the perfect spirits of the blessed can carry their bodies whither they please, and place them where they please?'[87] Augustine points out that a soul experiences weight quite differently from the way a body does for 'The soul carries the bodily members better when they are big and strong than when they are small and meagre; and whereas a big sound man is heavier to others' shoulders than a lean sick man, yet he will move his healthy heaviness with far more agility than the other can do his infirm lightness . . . Thus the state of the constitution is of more importance than great weight in considering our mortal, earthly and corruptible bodies. And who can describe the infinite difference between our present health and our future immortality?'[88] The final argument which Augustine declares he will not even mention, but of course immediately does, is that since the whole earth hangs alone without support there really is no grounds for doubting the ability of an earthly body also to stay up in heaven without support.

Augustine puts forward another argument in a third chapter entitled 'Against the wise men of the world that hold it impossible for man's body to be transported up to the dwellings of joy in heaven.'[89] In this he asserts that, in our present existence, souls which by nature belong to heaven live enclosed in earthly bodies. He then argues that if souls can come down to earth to be united to earthly bodies, why should it not be equally feasible for bodies to go up to heaven to be united with heavenly souls?

As far as I can see no other Father tackles these problems in this fullness. Nevertheless several Fathers talk of our ascension upwards,[90] and the majority explicitly locate our future abode in heaven,[91] so it is probably safe to assume that they would have used arguments similar to those of Augustine if they had ever felt the need to articulate their faith.[92]

Rufinus briefly mentions the problem of staying up. He makes use of St Paul's statement to the Thessalonians that we will be taken up into the clouds:[93] 'the flesh of the saints is to be gloriously transformed, being suspended in the clouds and carried along in the air to meet God ... There is no absurdity in the suggestion that the bodies of the saints will be raised up on clouds.'[94] Rufinus goes on to mention a composite biblical quotation that the 'Just shall shine as the sun, and as the brightness of the firmament, in the kingdom of God',[95] and deduces from this the idea that 'we will be adorned with the splendour of these stars',[96] an idea which was later to be developed in popular mediaeval Christianity into the idea that the stars were the souls of the Christian dead, and that a new star appeared whenever a person died.[97]

Origen is certainly much more aware of the difficulties of talking about a localised heaven than the other Fathers:

> there is no doubt that the Saviour alludes to something more glorious and splendid that this present world, and invites and exhorts all who believe in him to direct their course towards it. But whether that world, which he wishes us to know of, is one that stands widely apart and separate from this in space and quality and glory, or whether, as seems to me more likely, it excels in quality and glory but is nevertheless within the limits of this world is uncertain, and in my opinion an unsuitable subject for the mind and thoughts of men.[98]

Despite these mental reservations he does hesitantly say

> If anyone is pure in heart ... he will quickly ascend to the region of the air, until he reaches the kingdom of the heavens, passing through the series of those 'abiding places' ... which the Greeks have termed 'spheres' ... but which the divine scriptures calls heavens ... When the saints have reached the heavenly places, then they will see clearly the nature of the stars, one by one ... And when they have gone through everything connected with the reason of the stars and with those ways of life that exist in heaven they will come to the 'things which are not seen.'[99]

Origen believes that 'the things that are not seen' refer to a sphere beyond the 'spheres' of the planets, and 'above that sphere which is called fixed.' In this ultimate sphere lies 'an abiding place for the pious and blessed, in as it were a "good land" and a "land of the living", which "the meek" and gentle will receive for an inheritance. To this land belongs that heaven which, with its more magnificent circuit, surrounds and confines it, and this is the true heaven and the first to be so called.'[100]

These examples show that despite enormous differences of emphasis all the Fathers supposed that our bodies would, after appropriate transformation, ascend to an abode of the blessed in the sky. Indeed when a newspaper cartoonist portrays the next life in terms of a man with wings standing on a cloud, he is in fact combining the explanations of Augustine and Rufinus as to how we manage to stay up there. We have seen too that even Origen, the most sophisticated of the Fathers, hesitantly and reluctantly affirmed ascension to a land in the sky as our ultimate destiny.

It is not really necessary even to point out that the cosmological discoveries of the 17th Century have so thoroughly shattered this scheme of things that it is exceedingly hard for us even to comprehend that this is what talk of heaven meant throughout most of the Christian centuries. As we shall see in the next chapter, those who wish to affirm belief in a physical heaven must locate this 'heaven' either in a distant galaxy or in another space altogether. This has important implications for any notion of re-constituted and re-animated corpses going there after transformation.

For men ignorant of all the implications of gravity and of the problems of air supply in the upper atmosphere, it seemed possible to imagine that a minor modification such as wings sprouting from the shoulders might enable us to fly upwards to a relatively near abode in the sky.[102] Clouds could also be thought of as agencies for our ascension,[103] or even ladders like the one in Jacob's dream.[104] But there is no way one could make use of such suggestions to enable a resurrected body to move to another galaxy. A similar difficulty arises if we locate heaven in another space for it is part of the concept of 'another space' that nothing material can pass from one such space to another. Hence there seems to be no way belief in the resurrection of the corpse from the grave can today be combined with belief in its subsequent transference to any thinkable heaven.

A parallel argument can be used concerning the Fathers' expectation concerning the fate of the resurrected bodies of the wicked. They supposed that these would be transferred to everlasting punishment in hell,[105] which they located in the centre of the earth.[106] They assumed that the damned would burn there for ever without being consumed for, as both Augustine and Minucius Felix noted, the fires of Etna and Vesuvius burn continuously without being consumed,[107] and as Tertullian points out, "Volcanoes are the vent-holes of hell."[108] On this basis it seemed reasonable to suppose that the lake of fire underneath the earth would always burn but never consume the bodies of the damned.[109] The Fathers' observations were of course faulty, for the molten lava in a volcano is not burning, merely red-hot. But the point at issue is that it is unthinkable in the light of what we know about the earth's structure to suppose that its centre could provide a suitable location for the endless punishment of wicked human beings.

One might feel that the whole concept of hell would be unthinkable in the light of contemporary understanding of the purpose of punishment, and in the light of current thought concerning the central themes of the Christian gospel and of the doctrine of God as love, but a survey of the views of third year students at the Universities of Oxford, Cambridge and Bangor shows that 9 per cent of the total, and 30 per cent of regular worshippers, do believe in hell.[110] To this 30 per cent the question of hell's location, and how resurrected bodies are supposed to get there, should be as real a question as that of heaven's situation. I suggest that once again the only valid alternatives are another galaxy or another space, and once more I argue that there is no way resurrected corpses can get to either of these destinations after their emergence from the grave. A similar argument of course applies to those who reject the traditional concept of hell but, like Origen and Gregory of Nyssa,[111] hold that there must be some place which would provide opportunity for further growth, development, and purification, before a person is fitted for the full relationship with God hoped for in heaven.

I conclude that belief in the resurrection of the flesh is untenable today and therefore that modern Christians are right to discard it, not only because the patristic arguments in its favour have been discredited, but also because fleshly resurrection seems incompatible with the deeper intuition that in a future life we should progress beyond the limitation of our earthly existence to a new and better existence in heaven. Let us therefore turn now to consider how modern Christian thinkers have sought to re-interpret the notion of bodily resurrection in ways which do not require precise physical continuity.

# 4 John Hick's Theory of the Divine Creation of an Exact Replica

From earliest times there have been Christians who have been dissatisfied with the dominant belief in fleshly resurrection. As I sought to show in Chapter 2, St Paul's denial that flesh and blood could inherit eternal life seems to indicate that whatever he may have meant by 'resurrection', it did not entail the revivification of the corpse. And the fact that the creeds of the Eastern Church talk of 'resurrection of the dead', or of 'the body', indicates a persisting unease with the somewhat 'crude' understanding of bodily identity prevalent in the western Church. Certainly the proponents of fleshly resurrection suspected the reticence of their eastern brethren. Jerome even accused them of deliberate ambiguity: 'They use the word "body", instead of the word "flesh", in order that an orthodox person hearing them say "body" may take them to mean "flesh", while a heretic will understand that they mean "spirit".'[1] Jerome is unfair in making this assertion, since even Origen claimed to believe in the resurrection of the 'same body'[2] in explicit contrast to the purely spiritual and non-bodily future life expected by his opponent Celsus[3], and, as we saw in the last chapter, Origen located heaven in the sky. Nevertheless it remains true that the difference in the characteristic wording of western and eastern creeds does represent a significant variation of emphasis in their understanding of what it means to be a person. It is possible also that Cranmer's deliberate mistranslation of 'carnis' by 'body' may indicate that he too felt uneasy about the uncompromisingly materialistic concept of identity implied by the doctrine of fleshly resurrection.

M.E. Dahl has put forward a most interesting new way of approaching the concept of bodily resurrection. He suggests that we should interpret St Paul's position as teaching that 'Although the resurrection body will not be materially identical with the one we now possess, it will be somatically identical.'[4] 'Somatic identity' describes that continuous bodily identity which we recognise our friends as possessing, despite the fact that their constituent parts are in a continuous state of flux. For example, the Bishop of Ely is somatically identical with the man who was Principal of Westcott House seven years ago. But he is not materially identical, in that not one cell of his body has remained from his earlier state. Origen recognised this when he said that the body in its true meaning cannot be understood in terms of its contemporary component particles and compared it to a river, for as the water departs and the river remains, so the particles composing a body depart and the body remains.[5] Origen believed that the body is the same not by material continuity but by the permanence of that which gives the law, the *ratio*, of its constitution.[6]

St Thomas Aquinas adopted a position very close to Dahl's 'somatic identity' when he argued that the precise particles of which a body is composed form part of its accidents. It is the substance that will be restored at the resurrection and not necessarily all the accidents. 'He adduces various arguments to show why this must include hair, nails, 'humours', blood, and so forth, but that it will not include material identity of particles.'[7] In spite of the very strong emphasis Aquinas places on the resurrection of 'the same' body, he insists that the identity is 'specific, not numerical'.[8]

These ways of thinking about the nature of bodily identity are much more acceptable to modern thought than the 'identical structure' view. A.M. Ramsey points out: 'Today ... there is a tendency ... to hold that the persistence of a body lies not in the immutability of its physical constituents but in their continued organization in accordance with the principle of the body's self-identity.'[9] This assessment is supported by the interpretation of bodily identity given by the cyberneticist Norbert Wiener. John Hick summarises his position thus:

Wiener has graphically emphasised the non-dependence of

human bodily identity through time upon the identity of the physical matter momentarily composing the body. He points out that the living human body is not a static entity but a pattern of change: 'the individuality of the body is that of a flame rather than that of a stone, of a form rather than of a bit of substance.' As a pattern, the body can be regarded as a message that is in principle capable of being coded, transmitted, and then translated back into its original form.[10]

What is important about each of these ways of expressing our bodily identity is that none of them interpret resurrection of the body as requiring the material reconstitution of the actual dead body. If God were to create a 'replica' of a dead person, then as long as this divinely created 'replica' possessed the same 'somatic' identity (Dahl), or the same 'seminal principle or form' (Origen),[11] or the same 'substance' (in Aquinas' use of the word), or the same 'organising principle' (Ramsey), or the same 'code' (Wiener), it would be the same person though possessing no material continuity with the deceased person.

This way of understanding personal identity seems to lie behind Hick's suggestion about how we might think of bodily resurrection today. He suggests that we should think of it as 'The divine creation in another space of an exact psycho-physical "replica" of the deceased person.'[12] His reference to 'another space' may be regarded as equivalent to a spatial 'heaven'. Hick argues that the Resurrection World may be located in another space which is in no way related to our own. Austin Farrer defends this theory very strongly:

According to Einstein's unanswerable reasoning, space is not an infinite pre-existent field or area in which bits of matter float about. Space is a web of interactions between material energies which form a system by thus interacting. Unless the beings or energies of which heaven is composed are of a sort to interact physically with the energies in our physical world, heaven can be as dimensional as it likes, without ever getting pulled into our spatial field, or having any possible contact with us of any physical kind.[13]

Farrer's conclusions are supported by Anthony Quinton's defence of the conceivability of plural spaces in his article 'Spaces and Times' (*Philosophy*, April 1962). Hick defines plural spaces thus: 'The possibility of two spaces is the possibility of two sets of extended objects such that each member of each set is spatially related to each other member of the same set but not spatially related to any member of the other set. Thus everything in the space in which I am is at a certain distance and in a certain direction from me, and vice versa; but if there is a second space, nothing in it is at any further distance, or in any direction, from where I am now. In other words, from my point of view the other space is nowhere and therefore does not exist. But if there *is* a second space, unobservable by me, the objects in it are entirely real to an observer within that space, and our world is to him nowhere — not at any distance nor in any direction, so that from his point of view it does not exist.'[14].

This concept of plural spaces and times seems to be a coherent and reasonable theory, but I do not believe it will help our present hypothesis. For neither the arguments of Quinton nor Farrer fit the situation we are now envisaging.

Quinton's argument points out that in our dreams we experience spatial and temporal entities and happenings which cannot be located within our normal space-time perceptions. Yet the entities within our dreams may well be coherently spatially related to each other, and likewise the events which take place may follow each other in a coherent temporal sequence. The dreamed-of tiger is nowhere near my bed, and from the point of view of my normal perception the tiger is not at any distance, nor in any direction from where I am sleeping. Further, although I dream at night, the tiger is prowling in the midday sun, and although I dreamed for ten minutes, the tiger hunt lasted all day. So neither the times nor the places can be related.[15]

This is an important argument, for one can go on to postulate many different worlds all existing in the consciousness of God, or even in the consciousness of individual minds. I hope to develop such arguments later when expounding H.H. Price's idea of a purely mental existence. It is as Hick rightly says, 'logically possible for there to be any number of worlds, each its own space, these worlds being all observed by the universal consciousness of God but only one of them being observed by an embodied being who is part of one of those worlds.'[16]

But although there may be many other worlds they owe their reality to their existence in the mind of God, as Berkeley thought this world did. However, it is not generally held that Berkeley's philosophy adequately describes the actuality of our present world,[17] and what we are discussing is the possibility of an exact psycho-physical 'replica' of a body which *ex hypothesi* belongs to this present non-Berkeleyan world. Unless therefore we suppose that I am at present only an idea in the mind of God, an exact 'replica' of what I am now cannot be only an idea in the mind of God. Hence Quinton's argument cannot support the thesis that my body might continue to exist in another space, at best it indicates only the possibility of mental survival.

Farrer's position, based on modern physics rather than philosophy, will not help us either. According to Farrer, there are important limitations on the sort of worlds which can exist in their own physical space. 'There is no need to support that heaven falls somewhere in the field of space . . . unless the beings or energies of which it is composed are of a sort to interact physically with the energies in our physical world.'[18] In Farrer's understanding of heaven this condition is fulfilled; 'Obviously heaven is dimensional: but the stuff of glory which composes its constituents is surely not apt to interact with sticks and stones, with flesh and blood.'[19] The same is not true of Hick's 'other space', for an exact psycho-physical 'replica' requires a physical world in which time, distance, matter and energy interact in the same way as in our own. But though there may be any number of dimensions and any number of different spaces, there cannot be two space-time systems subject to the same physical laws for two such systems could not avoid being spatially related. I conclude therefore that the existence of plural spaces and times is a logical possibility and hence Farrer's heaven may exist, but not Hick's exactly similar 'other-space.'

If my conclusion is valid what consequences follow for

Professor Hick's suggestions about the resurrection of the body? I suggest that his basic argument is unaffected. Instead of postulating 'another space' we postulate 'another place'. Thus we suppose that the divine creation of exact replicas takes place 'on a planet of some other star,'[20] for as Hick stated in his original version of this theory, 'It is not essential to the notion of a resurrection world that its space should have properties different from those of physical space.' However, he moved to the postulation of 'another space' because 'most of those who consider the question reject as absurd the possibility of, for example, radio communication or rocket travel between earth and heaven.'[21] This is an important objection because it does seem religiously important that between heaven and earth there should be 'a great gulf fixed' so that none may pass from heaven to earth or vice versa (cf. Luke 16/26). There seems something very bizarre in even the possibility of an astronaut meeting an exact replica of his deceased grandfather on some interplanetary excursion.

However, this consequence can be avoided if we suppose that the resurrection world is in some other galaxy. The nearest galaxy to us is M.31 Nebula in Andromeda, at a distance of two million light years;[22] a 'great enough gulf' to rule out any possibility of travel from this world to the next, because almost all writers seem to accept the speed of light as the outside limit, and I am convinced by N.J. Berrill's argument that 'time-dilation through relativistic theory has meaning only in the mathematico-physical world and that organisms age according to their local time-systems.'[23] Further we may add that if two million light years distance were thought to be too close, there are a thousand million theoretically observable galaxies at vastly greater distances, to say nothing of whatever galaxies there may be beyond the range of any telescope, and to ignore the fact that the most distant galaxies appear to be receding from us at speeds increasingly approaching the speed of light.[24]

I believe that a distance of two million light years is quite sufficient to ensure that no possible interaction could ever take place and that for all practical purposes everything that Hick says about another space could be equally well applied to a planet of a star in another galaxy. Such a planet 'would be unobservable by me' (since we cannot even see whether the nearest star at 4.3 light-years has a planet,[25] let alone a star in another galaxy). But despite its unobservability, the 'objects in it would be entirely real to an observer' on that planet; 'our own planet would be to him nowhere' and 'from his point of view would not exist.' Hence I believe that nothing whatever would be lost from defining Hick's theory of the resurrection as 'the divine creation in another *place* of an exact psycho-physical "replica" of the deceased person.'

But can the 'replica' be regarded as the same person as the one who had previously died?

Hick defends the appropriateness of our making such an identification by presenting three progressively odd, but logically possible, cases for our consideration. First he pictures a man disappearing in the midst of some learned gathering in England and an exact 'replica' being spontaneously created and appearing at a similar meeting in New York. The 'replica' in New York is in every physical and psychological detail identical to the man who disappeared. 'There is continuity of memory, complete similarity of bodily features, including fingerprints, hair and eye colouration and stomach contents, and also of beliefs, habits, and mental propensities.'[26] Hick invites us to imagine that a deputation of his colleagues in England fly to New York and find the 'replica' in every respect 'but one exactly as though he had travelled from London to New York by conventional means. The only difference is that he describes how, as he was listening to Dr Z reading a paper, on blinking his eyes he suddenly found himself sitting in a different room listening to a different paper by an American scholar.'[27] Hick believes that in such a situation all concerned would rapidly come to accept that the 'replica' was in fact to be identified with the man who so strangely disappeared.

The second picture is even odder, for we are asked to 'suppose that the event in London is not a sudden and inexplicable disappearance but a sudden death. Only, at the moment when the individual dies a 'replica' of him as he was at the moment before his death, and complete with memory up to that instant, comes into existence in New York. Even with the corpse on our hands it would still ... be an extension of 'same person' required and warranted by the postulated facts to say that the one who died has been miraculously re-created in New York.' Hick pictures all the circumstantial details surrounding the case and concludes, 'the factors inclining us to say that the one who died and the one who appeared are the same person would far outweigh the factors inclining us to say that they are different people.'[28]

In both these cases one of the most convincing reasons for identifying the 'replica' with the man who disappeared or the man who died was that the 'replica' possessed the memory and self-awareness of his former life. Indeed, without such memory and self-awareness he would probably not be accepted as being the former person, especially in the case where there was the added complication of the corpse. This consideration is important when we come to Hick's third picture of a man dying on earth and of his 'replication' on the planet of a star in another galaxy (my modification of Hick's 'another space'). If we were prepared to accept the identification of a New York 'replica' with a man who died in London, then likewise, we should accept that a divinely created 'replica' in another galaxy should also be regarded as being the man who died. But in this third case we are not in a position to do the identifying. The only person there involved would be the man who died and possibly some other 'replicas' of people 'he' had known during 'his' earthly life, who would recognise 'him' after his re-creation. From the point of view of the individual who died there would be no question of 'his' continuing existence. If I die on earth and at that moment an exact psycho-physical replica of me came into being on a planet in Andromeda possessing all my memories and self-awareness then that 'replica' must be me. For by the word 'me' I mean the owner of my memories, my bodily frame, and my self-awareness. Even if one regards the concept of 'ownership' as loaded, the argument still holds. It can be expressed as 'I am my memories, my body and my self-awareness.' Further I know my body as my body, not through knowledge of its material constituency, but through knowledge of the way it looks to me and of the way it habitually functions. I could not distinguish in any way between my body and an exact psycho-physical replica of my body which I found myself inhabiting.

Hick describes how the life of the newly created 'replica' might be experienced. He uses the first person because if my 'replica' actually possesses my memories it can only think of itself as being me. 'I have the experience of waking up from unconsciousness as I have on other occasions woken up from sleep', and I am no more inclined in the one case than the other, to doubt my own identity as an individual persisting through time. I realise, either immediately or presently, that I have died, both because I can remember being on my death bed and because my environment is now different and is populated by people some of whom I know to have died. Evidences of this kind could mount up to the point at which they are quite as strong as the evidence, which, in the previous two pictures, convince the individual in question that he has been miraculously translated to New York. Resurrected persons would be individually no more in doubt about their own identity than we are now, and would presumably be able to identify one another in the same kinds of ways and with a like degree of assurance as we do now.'[29]

I find Hick's sequence of pictures convincing and I believe that they do establish the bare logical possibility of interpreting resurrection in terms of re-creation on another planet in another galaxy. But one difficulty has been raised against the hypothesis. This is 'the spectre of two or more identical resurrection Mr Xs.' The argument runs thus:

> If it makes sense to suppose that God might create a second-space reproduction of Mr C, then it makes sense to suppose that he might create two or more such second-space reproductions. However, since X2 and X3 would then each be the same person as X1 (deceased), they would then each be the same person; which is absurd. Thus the existence of X3, or even the logical possibility of X3, prevents us from identifying X2 with X1.[30]

This objection is based on a faulty premise. It simply does not follow that 'if it makes sense for God to create a

second-space reproduction of Mr X, *then* it makes sense for
God to create two or more such . . . reproductions.' Hick's
article is an attempt to spell out how we can 'intelligibly
think of the resurrection of the body today.' The ground on
which belief in bodily resurrection is based is the faith that
each individual person is unique and precious in the sight of
God. According to Harnack 'the infinite value of the human
soul'[31] (which in this context means 'personality') was one of
the most fundamental of all the teachings of Jesus. And in no
doctrine is the importance of the individual so spelt out as in
the doctrine of bodily resurrection. William Barclay in his
commentary on the Apostle's creed sums up the essence of
this clause: 'The real truth behind the idea of the resurrection
of the body is that the individual survives as an individual.'[32]
Leonard Hodgson is even more clear on this connection: 'Our
hope of a future life is grounded in the conviction that the
creative process would make nonsense of itself if it stopped
short of fulfilling the end for which it has been individuali-
sing human beings as persons'.[33] "In order to make sense of
the Universe we must postulate the continuance of personal
life after death. In Christ, God reveals Himself as the God
who takes the action which confirms this postulate and
makes sense of what would otherwise be nonsensical."[34] In
short, the grounds for Christian belief in resurrection stem
from particular beliefs about the character of God, the
purpose of God in creation, and the worth in the sight of
God of each individual human being. In this context of belief
it makes sense to suppose that God may make provision for
each person to grow and develop after death in some other
world or mode of being and hence for God to make a replica
of him. But there are no grounds in this argument which
would make a second or third replica either necessary or
desirable. Hence the argument 'if one — then two or three' is
not valid. Moreover, even if the premise has been valid the
conclusion would not have followed for as Hick points
out:'The fact that if there were two or more Mr Xs none of
them would be Mr X, does not prevent there being the only
kind of Mr 'X' that could exist, namely a single one.'[35]

   A second objection to Hick's theory is his use of the word
'exact' to qualify the psycho-physical 'replica' of the

deceased person. Unamended, this poses an insuperable problem to the theory for, as Hick himself acknowledges, 'an exact "replica" of a dying man at his last moment of life would be a dying man at his last moment of life! In other words, the first thing that the resurrection body would do is to expire.'[36] One solution to the problem might be to suppose that the "replica" should be an exact copy of the deceased at an earlier stage of his life when he was still enjoying good health and vitality, at the age of thirty or so. But the disadvantage of this suggestion would be that 'he will presumably lose in the resurrection all the memories and all the development of character that had accrued to him on earth since that age.'[37]

Hick's own solution to this problem is to suggest that we think of the resurrection body as being created 'at the last moment of conscious personal life. And then, instead of its immediately or soon dying, we must suppose that in its new environment it is subjected to processes of healing and repair which bring it into a state of health and activity. In the case of old people ... we might even conceive of a process of growing physically younger to an optimum age.'[38] This solution is subject to two fatal objections. First, a body growing daily younger would have to be composed of some type of matter so unlike the material of which our bodies are at present composed that such a body could not be described as an exact replica. Secondly many in the west die after prolonged hospitalisation. Stravinsky, for example, spent four fully conscious years in an intensive care unit, dependent for survival on a variety of machines, drips, tubes and injections. If we posit a gradual and natural process of healing in the resurrection world, we must assume a standard of medical technology at least equal to ours in order to look after the newly replicated people during their initial period of healing. But why should their medical technology be equal to ours? The knowledge which they carried with them from their previous lives on earth would probably be up to a generation behind the latest techniques. We can suggest that after their own recovery the doctors among them resumed their earthly medical research with growing youthfulness and vigour added to the experience of a completed life-time. But what motivation could they have had for their researches living in an environment in which they were not victims to the degenerative diseases of old age and in which everyone 'youthed' to an optimum age? What happened we may ask to the *first* man who died on earth after living for months in a heart-lung machine? The doctors in the resurrection world would not have known of this invention from their own experience on earth and they would have had no need to invent one in the resurrection world. Yet an exact replica of a man who had spent many months on such a machine could not survive without it for the necessary period of healing and rejuvenation in the resurrection world.

The problems magnify as we consider them: presumably my heart pace-maker and artificial knee joint are replicated with me, but what about my glasses and false teeth? Do limbs amputated years ago grow again during the process of healing? What about the thalidomide victim whose limbs never grew? What about the Siamese twin who died eighteen hours before his brother to whom he had been joined for all his life? Did he wait for his brother before being re-created? If so, he was not an exact replica for he would have to have possessed a complete organ which he had never had during his life. Were the twins re-created in the joined-together state they were in when the first twin died, or were they re-created as the separate entities they were when the second died on the following day?

I believe these arguments are fatal, not to the theory as a whole, but to Hick's use of the word 'exact', which I believe can be omitted without affecting the basic position. The doctrine of man on which Hick's theory is based is not the old patristic one that a man is his present component particles but on more sophisticated theories of what it means to be a person, such as theories of 'somatic identity', 'form', 'substance', 'organising principle' or 'pattern capable of being coded.' In everyday life we experience our bodies as characteristically ours when they are healthy. Thus a sick man will report 'I don't feel myself today', and others will say of him 'He's not at all himself.' This linguistic usage reflects the intuition most of us have that we are most fully ourselves when our physical and mental powers are functioning properly. St Augustine articulates this feeling when he says: 'In animal bodies . . . sickness and wounds are nothing but the privation of health. When a cure is effected the evils which were present (i.e. the sickness and the wounds) do not retreat and go elsewhere. Rather they simply do not exist any more. For such evil is not a substance; the wound or the disease is a defect of the bodily substance which, as a substance is good.[39] Farrer echoes this statement: 'Disease is not its own way of being; it is the breakdown of health.'[40]

A bodily hurt or disease is not essential either to our understanding of ourselves or to others' recognition of ourselves. For example, at the moment of writing this I am suffering from a sprained achilles' tendon. This, I suggest, is in every way 'accidental to me'. In dictionary terms it was 'An unexpected casualty or mishap' and it is 'A property or quality [of me] not essential to [my] conception of [myself].'[41] If Norbert Wiener wished to take down the pattern of my body in code and transmit me telegraphically to some distant place, I would expect him to code my achilles tendon as it should be, not as it is, and if God were to re-create me in some distant galaxy I would expect him to do likewise.

When the dying man moans 'I'm not myself', and his friends agree 'He's not himself', it seems most perverse to insist that the only self either he or his friends could recognise as him in a resurrection world should be that very self he and they have repudiated in this. Hence I would suggest that the word 'exact' should be removed as the qualifier of 'replica', and perhaps the idea of 'substantial' (in the Aristotelian sense) substituted. This would be an awkward word to use because of its other connotations in modern English. I suggest therefore that we use Dahl's expression and describe the resurrection bodies as being 'somatically identical.' This expression is intended to convey that the re-creation person was truly 'of one substance' with the deceased in that the re-created person was a 'replica' of the deceased's body and soul functioning together perfectly in a new life. The essence of the resurrection doctrine is that it is the complete man who conquors death and lives as a complete man not subject to the 'accidental' maiming or disease which the deceased actually endured. If we can believe in our re-creation from that total disease and maiming which we experience in death, then it is reasonable to suppose that our re-creation would also involve our res-toration from such disease and maiming as occurred before our final illness, and even that our restoration from such disease and maiming as occurred while we were still in our mothers' wombs.

I present therefore the hypothesis of divine creation in another galaxy of a psycho-physical 'replica' somatically identical with the deceased person. I believe that this theory is logically possible and presents an intelligible account of how the resurrection might be understood today. The possibility is permanently unverifiable during earthly life and therefore can be no more than a bare logical possibility which may or may not be confirmed by post-mortem experience.

What we can ask however, is whether the logical possibility is at all likely, and whether it is something we might expect a reasonable and loving God to bring about. To answer these questions we need to attempt to visualise how this re-creation would work out in practice.

The nature of the issues involved will vary, depending on whether we assume resurrection life to be temporary or permanent, reproductive or sterile. Let us start with the orthodox Christian belief in 'The resurrection of the body and the life ever-lasting.'[42] This applies to all men the words which St Paul applied to Jesus, 'Christ being raised from the dead dieth no more. Death hath no more dominion over him.'[43] One problem facing such belief is that, as our resurrection bodies are *ex hypothesi* to be somatically identical to our present ones, we must live on a planet of the same approximate size as our present earth or gravity would be too great for us to function effectively. This causes serious problems, for no planet of comparable size to our own could support more than a few generations of earth's dead. This would mean that over the past five hundred thousand years or so[44] many hundreds of planets must have been colonised by re-created earthmen and hundreds more planets will be colonised in the years that may lie ahead.

However, the conditions under which man can survive are extremely limited and planets possessing the appropriate bio-sphere are often thought to be extremely rare.[45]

We are to suppose that on one of these planets, namely this earth, man evolved, whereas on hundreds of other such planets scattered over thousands of galaxies this incredibly rare environment evolved with all the necessary vegetable and animal life to sustain man but with no indigenous hominoid population. And all this happened so that one day these other planets would be able to receive re-created earthmen who would drop out of the blue and live there for ever and ever. I believe that this is what everlasting bodily resurrection entails and I find it incredible.

But let me suspend my disbelief and explore the concept of everlasting bodily life still further. The problems swiftly multiply: no planet will last forever, and nor could any human body. It is true that G. Rattray Taylor believes that human bodily aging could be stopped or reversed,[46] but nothing it seems could ever stop the slow death of a human brain.[47] However, 'with God all things are possible,'[48] so let us suppose that by divine fiat both person and planet endure. We then face the further problem of whether man could actually enjoy responsible free life in a real physical world without being open to the possibility that at some stage he might suffer accidental or malicious damage leading to death, or maiming. I believe that, as long as men are men, the possibility of death or maiming could not be excluded without postulating constant divine intervention to preserve men from the consequences of human folly or sin. But such action on God's part would take from us the responsibility for our own actions and thereby diminish our status as moral beings. Hick's comments about life in a world in which suffering was impossible could be applied to this situation: 'If one man tried to murder another, his bullet would melt innocuously into thin air, or the blade of his knife turn to paper . . . Anyone driving at break-neck speed along a narrow road and hitting a pedestrian would leave his victim miraculously unharmed; or if anyone slipped and fell through a fifth-floor window, gravity would be partially suspended and he would float gently to the ground.'[49] Such a world would not be as conducive to the development of character and responsibility or for spiritual growth as is life in this present world with all its challenges, uncertainties and dangers. Yet the religious motivation for believing in a future life is that there we grow and mature as persons until we achieve 'the measure of the stature of the fulness of Christ.'[50] St Peter believed that after our brief suffering we would be 'restored, established, and strengthened on a firm foundation', and that 'the God of all grace would call [us] into his eternal glory.'[51] The New Testament hope is not for an everlasting and undying restoration of our present bodily existence, but rather that we may be prepared for 'An eternal weight of glory beyond all comparison.'[52] Hence I reject the idea of ever-lasting continuance of our present somatic identity as not only incredible, but as religiously pointless.

However, this does not rule out the possibility that there may be a resurrection world into which we are re-created, but for a life of limited duration, after which we proceed to further developments in other worlds, or possibly in other modes of being.

Such a concept would be in accordance with the wide-spread Christian belief that life after death should provide opportunity for growth, purification and spiritual advance.

Hick has argued that such a belief is a logical necessity if 'God's purpose of the perfecting of human beings is ever to be fulfilled.' 'For our sanctification — that is to say, our perfecting as persons — is . . . still radically incomplete' at the moment of death. If it were brought to 'instantaneous completion by divine fiat' it would seem

> far from clear that an individual who had been instan-taneously perfected would be in any morally significant sense the same person as the frail erring mortal who had lived and died. It would seem more proper to say, not that this previously very imperfect person has now become perfect, but that he had ceased to exist and that a perfect individual has been created in his place. But if we are thus to be transmuted in the twinkling of an eye into perfect creatures, the whole earthly travail of faith and moral effort is rendered needless. For God might by an exercise of omnipotence have created us as . . . perfect creatures in the first place. That he has not done so suggests that the nature of finite personal life requires that man's sanc-

tification takes place at every stage through his own response and assent, and that the process of man's free interaction with divine grace cannot be bypassed. And this in turn points to the conception of a continued life in an intermediate state.[53]

Let us therefore ask whether divine re-creation of a somatically identical 'replica' of the deceased person for a life of limited duration on another planet in another galaxy would be suitable as the next stage in our development. The problems differ depending upon whether we assume the next life to be reproductive or sexually sterile. Some might quote Jesus' teaching, 'At the resurrection men and women do not marry, but are like angels in heaven.'[54] This is not strictly relevant because we are discussing the recreation of our present somatic identity on another planet, and not an angel-like existence in heaven. But because so many Patristic writers[55] assume that bodily resurrection will be sexless, let us explore what the consequences of this would be. Since *ex hypothesi* we are to be recreated with our earthly memories, dispositions and behavioural patterns, and with our hormonal structure and physical health restored to an ideal fitness, a non-marital and non-sexual society would involve considerable psychological adjustment. The question is not simply that 'being no longer enslaved to the lusts of the flesh'[56] (Irenaeus), we would 'withdraw our virility from intercourse'[57] (Tertullian) and 'enjoy another's beauty without lust'[58] (Augustine), for the issues do not involve sexual restraint alone, but our total life style. Most people are accustomed to live in a marital home, and would not think of setting up monastic institutions on arrival on another planet. The Fathers did not see this problem, because they thought of a celibate and monastic existence as the ideal style of life.[59] But I submit that the average person brought up in a modern western society and sharing our present understanding of sex and family life, would not be the *same person* if in a next world he chose an institutional and a-sexual existence. Sociological evidence demands that we should give 'recognition to the secular reality of marriage as an almost universal way of life for men and women.'[60]

According to the Archbishop's Commission on Marriage, 'God has acted throughout the natural sequence of events which has moulded the nature and being of *homo sapiens, so* that for most people the need for marriage is built into their being.'[61] Modern psychological study has shown that our sexuality is an important part of our somatic identity.[62] I argue therefore that a non-marital and sexless resurrection world would be incompatible with the belief that the men and women to be re-created there would be somatically identical to the men and women now living on earth.

A further objection to a sexless resurrection world is that it would not be as conducive to personal development and growth as life on this present earth. The Archbishop's Commission states: 'Marriage is one of the central means through which the continuation of the development of the personality occurs.'[63] 'Marriage, considered not merely sexually but also in its psychological aspects, can meet the deepest human needs because it contains the basic ingredients of a relationship within which each partner can discover himself or herself through the other, and each can offer to the other the opportunity for healing and growth on the basis of progressive mutual completion.'[64] The responsibilities of parenthood in creating a happy, stable home and in caring for the physical, emotional, social and spiritual requirements of their children may also bring out qualities of character, compassion and reliability which can enhance and deepen the human person. Hick writes 'The most mature and valuable form of love in human life is the love between a man and a woman upon which the family is built ... And it is hard to see how such love could ever be developed in human life, in this its deepest and most valuable form of mutual sharing, except in an environment which has much in common with our own world.'[65] I suggest that the 'environment' of the resurrection world would need to include a setting in which love, marriage and family life could exist, for although the single state can be for some the way to personal development and fulfilment, 'marriage is, without question, the vocation of the great majority'.[66] Hence I reject a sexless resurrection, because it is not only impossible if we are to retain our present somatic identity, but also because it would be non-conducive to the purposes for which we suppose a temporary future life may exist.

We now turn to the possibility that a resurrection world might include marriage and the subsequent procreation of children. Unfortunately for this theory however, a world in which the generations continuously succeed each other poses the same population problem as a world whose occupants never die. Once more no planet could support more than a few generations of earth's dead, so once more we must suppose that hundreds of planets have evolved a complex biosphere like our own in order that one day they might receive re-created earth men and women who, like Adam and Eve of biblical legend, would suddenly appear on an earth which had been created for their benefit and on which they would commence to propagate the human species. Such radical discontinuity in the evolutionary pattern of so many planets seems so unlikely that I cannot regard it as a reasonable belief. Yet the situation is even odder than this, for presumably the children of the re-created earthmen are not destined to die eternally and so we must postulate their re-creation on still further worlds, and their children on yet more. At each step the hypothesis grows more and more bizarre.

However, let us ask ourselves once more the question, even if such re-creation were practical, would it be desirable? Would it accord with what we might expect a loving and reasonable God to do? One consequence of re-creation at maturity with full memories of an earthly life is that the experience would have a most profound effect upon one's thinking. I would imagine that it would also cause much heart-searching in Christians as to what kind of God they believe in. Hick has argued that survival by itself would not necessarily vindicate theism. 'It might be taken as just a surprising natural fact.'[67] This seems confirmed by the fact that 10 per cent of atheists believe in immortality.[68]

But although some forms of survival may be compatible with atheism, I believe that re-creation on another planet would seem compelling proof of God's reality. Indeed I believe it would not only vindicate theism, but it might also re-open the question of the historicity of Adam and Eve, for

if man could be discontinuous with an otherwise evolutionary world elsewhere, then why not on this earth too? Or
indeed, if the other world did not evolve at all but was
specially created for the benefit of the re-created earthman,
then why not our own planet? In short, divine re-creation on
another planet might seem not merely to compel belief in
theism in general, but belief in a very fundamentalist God in
particular. Re-creation on another planet would seem such a
demonstration of divine power as to compel belief in at least
the power of God, and this might have a damaging effect
upon the nature of man's relationship with God. As Hick has
argued, it is a basic principle of the Christian awareness of
God that 'for the sake of creating a personal relationship of
love and trust with his human creatures, God does not force
an awareness of himself upon them.'[69] It is true that
awareness of God's creative power is not in itself grounds for
loving or trusting him, or supposing that any realtionship
with him is either desirable or possible. God might create life,
and re-create man, with the same attitude that a scientist in a
laboratory might have to what he had produced. Nevertheless
it is generally felt that certain knowledge of God's reality
might compel at least a prudential veneration of his power
inappropriate to a free, loving response to a dawning
consciousness of God's reality.

Hence I believe that re-creation on another planet might in
fact hinder, rather than encourage, a truly personal response
to the loving purpose of God, and inhibit our advance and
spiritual growth towards 'the glorious liberty of the sons of
God'.[70]

Consequently, although Hick's re-interpretation of what
bodily resurrection might mean is logically possible, I suggest
that it be rejected as an untenable hypothesis, not only
because of the immense practical difficulties to which I have
drawn attention, but also because it does not seem to be
something we might reasonably expect a loving God to bring
about.

# 5 The Resurrection of the Body in Modern Thought

The most common belief in a future life among contemporary Christians is that after death we will be given new and glorious bodies in heaven. These 'spiritual bodies' will not be the same bodies as those we now inhabit, nor will they be glorified and transformed versions of these bodies. Rather they will be quite different bodies, and the only bond of unity between our present and future bodies is that they will be 'owned' successively by the same personality.

In the Archbishop of Canterbury's Commission on *Doctrine in the Church of England* we read:

> We ought to reject quite frankly the literalistic belief in a future resuscitation of the actual physical frame which is laid in the tomb . . . none the less . . . in the life of the world to come the soul or spirit will still have its appropriate organ of expression and activity, which is one with the body of earthly life in the sense that it bears the same relation to the same spiritual entity. What is important when we are speaking of the identity of any person's 'body', is not its physico-chemical constitution, but its relation to that person.[1]

The Catechism compiled by the Roman Catholic Bishops of the Netherlands says: 'We must not think of the resurrection as a return to the flesh and blood of our mortal frame.'[2] 'This body of the resurrection is not molecules which are buried and scattered in the earth . . . man begins to awake as a new man.' After death we experience 'resurrection of the new body'.[3] It is true that a commisson of Cardinals has explicitly contradicted this and other teaching contained in this Dutch Catechism,[4] but according to Professor Hans Küng this only shows that contemporary theology 'has made practically no headway in the Curia.'[5] For the consensus of contemporary theological thinking endorses what M.E. Dahl describes as 'The Accepted Exegesis' of the New Testament evidence, which is that 'Christians . . . will not have their physical bodies restored in a glorified form but will be provided with new ones like their Lord's.'[6] That this is the most popular contemporary view can be shown by a random survey of books on Christian doctrine in current usage.

Concerning the relationship of our present and supposed future bodies: E.J. Bicknell and Michael Paternoster talk of 'physical discontinuity';[8] A.M. Ramsey denies 'material continuity';[8] C.B. Moss says that it is 'not the same body';[9] Norman Pittenger thinks it will not be a 'material body at all' and that 'the physics, chemistry and biology of our present bodies will not be involved'[10] John Austin Baker says that the resurrection body 'cannot be described in physical terms';[11] Russell Aldwinkle, Hugh Burnaby, and Wheeler Robinson[12] deny any continuance of our present bodies; Hugh Montefiore writes 'when we rise from the dead it won't have anything to do with our physical bodies';[13] John Baillie says: 'It is difficult to believe we would retain bodily organisms to all eternity';[14] Alec Vidler thinks 'that in eternity we shall possess spiritual organisms equivalent to, though different from, the physical bodies which we possess here and now';[15] David Winter says that we will have a 'new bodily vehicle'[16] and Charles Gore that we will be 'clothed with a new embodiment';[17] Leonard Hodgson says 'we cannot begin to think of what we mean by a spiritual body in terms of what it will look like, or be made of',[18] and Austin Farrer describes the resurrection body as 'a new gift of God',[19] and implies that it will have nothing in common with 'flesh and blood.'[20]

As to what replaces physical continuity as the unifying factor between the two bodies, these writers tend to be somewhat vague; Farrer[21] and Moss insist that there must be some relationship but confess, 'of what kind we do not know.'[22] The Dutch Catechism echoes this, talking of 'something of man which is most properly himself.'[23] The other writers use one or more of the following phrases: 'personality',[24] 'personal identity',[25] 'the persons we have become',[26] 'the full integrity of our humanity',[27] 'the vital principle of what we are',[28] 'the law or ratio of our constitution',[29] 'our formal identity',[30] 'our intelligence',[31] 'our memory traces and dispositions',[32] and 'our soul or spirit'.[33]

In short the eighteen writers I have mentioned above all share the view that there is an important sense in which I shall still be 'I', although destined to live in a totally new embodiment in a new kind of existence. However, not all exponents of Christian doctrine share this view. Biblical scholars like C.F.D. Moule,[34] G.B. Caird,[35] William Barclay,[36] and M. Carrey,[37] Conservative Evangelicals like J.A. Motyer,[38] and traditionalists like the Cardinals appointed to investigate the Dutch Catechism,[39] all argue for a real connection between our present physical bodies and the bodies of the resurrection. Professor Moule for instance thinks that the matter of which our present bodies are composed is 'ultimately used as the material of a new existence.'[40]

Other scholars like Oliver Quick and J.S. Whale find it hard to put into words what they really believe about the future life. Both are certain of its reality and importance, but Whale thinks that all descriptions are inadequate,[41] and Quick that 'theologians are still in quest of a metaphysic that will do justice to the Easter Gospel.'[42]

Finally of course there are Christian theologians like G. Kaufman who thinks that 'we have no reason to suppose that . . . life continues beyond the grave.'[43] Rudolph Bultmann goes further and describes the hope for a future life as 'not merely unintelligible to modern man, it is completely meaningless.'[44] This denial of any kind of personal continuance is not really affected by David Edwards' supposition that we shall live on in God's memory,[45] or in Paul Tillich's talk of God's eternity as distinct from the transitoriness of human life,[46] for neither Edwards nor Tillich believes that we will share either God's memory or his eternity.[47]

There would be obvious dangers in drawing any conclusions from a survey of only twenty-nine authors, were it not that the authors I have cited form a fairly representative cross-section of Christian thought. The works on doctrine are among those generally found on the shelves of most clergymen's studies, and the paperbacks on life after death are those currently available. So I think it not unreasonable to assume that these books reflect the current trends in contemporary Christian thinking, with the proviso that established works and popular paper-backs often lag behind the most modern approaches, and hence I suspect that Christian agnosticism concerning any kind of future life might be under-represented in such a sample. However, I think it safe to say that of Christian authors who do have a positive doctrine concerning a future life the overwhelming consensus favours the view that our personalities will be clothed with new bodies in heaven, and that it is only those who are steeped in the biblical world view who still wish to affirm a real material link between our present and future bodies.

Professor Moule believes that the stories of the empty tomb are 'early and doctrinally significant', and show

> the transformation of his [Jesus'] material body into 'a body' of a different kind. Jesus may also have anticipated some ultimate plan of God for using up matter into what is transmaterial . . . and it may be God's intention that the whole of matter should be thus transformed. The total transformation of Jesus indicated by the empty tomb would then be a sort of harbinger. If we believe in creation 'out of nothing', is there any reason why that which is created should not be used up 'into something' new? Fuel is transformed into energy. May not human personality be enabled by God's vitality, to turn matter into something permanent, and may not what Paul calls 'a spiritual body' be the beginning of this process for each individual? The matter which is manifestly 'left behind' at death may yet be intended to become part of some such transformation ultimately.[48]

Moule is conscious that 'this seems ludicrous — so ludicrous that one hardly dare formulate it. And yet what is the alternative? Only, I believe to capitulate either to leaving the empty tomb out of theological consideration or to accepting it as a symbol of time space involvement without, however, elucidating what that involvement implies.'[49] This is a most revealing comment. It shows that Moule is prepared to defend an idea which he finds ludicrous, simply because he is convinced that it is Biblical. This is an attitude of mind which I find very hard to understand, especially when it is manifested by so eminent a New Testament scholar who writes with full knowledge of the difficulties and ambiguities of the New Testament data in general, and of the Resurrection narratives in particular. I suggest that if an idea is ludicrous it must be rejected, no matter how Biblical it might, or might not, be.

There was nothing ludicrous in the authors of the second Epistle of Peter[50] and of the Revelation of St John expecting a new heaven and a new earth,[51] for to them this simply meant this earth and the land in the sky above this earth, and to the more educated of the Fathers it meant this earth and its surrounding 'spheres'. Further, both the New Testament writers and the early Fathers thought that this cosmos of earth and heaven had only been in existence since a historical genesis a few thousand years earlier. What could be more natural than that the God who had created this cosmos in the relatively recent past should also destroy and re-make it in the relatively near future? To a modern Christian however the Universe is vast beyond our powers of imagining, consists of countless millions of stars and planets, has been in existence in something like its present form for at least five thousand million years, and even the 'Big Bang' which perhaps launched the expanding Universe we now know may have been the product of a previous collapse.[52] Further, although Professor Robertson expects our present Universe to start contracting in upon itself again in 2,700 million years time,[53] this is far removed from the biblical 'end of the world' since even this collapse will presumably be the prelude to another 'Big Bang'. Long before that all life on our planet will have died out and our sun exploded as a red giant[54] or a super-nova.[55] Nothing of this, strictly speaking, prevents one continuing to believe that God may intervene and bring the whole thing to an end, but somehow it makes such belief seem bizarre. Supposing that the collapse of our present universe in 2,700 million years time was in fact the end, would it really make sense for God to search out the particles of matter from a long dead planet, absorbed millions of years previously in a super-nova explosion, and then use this matter to make a quite new spiritual body for me to inhabit in a new 'trans-material' existence? Besides, what does it mean for God to transform matter into something trans-material? Matter is defined by its place in the matter-energy-space-time equation of modern physics, $E = mc^2$, just as a triangle is defined by its possession of three sides. One can no more change matter into something trans-material than one can change a triangle into a square. To think otherwise is to ignore the fact that matter and energy form part of the same reality, and hence changing matter into energy is not a suitable analogy for changing matter into something trans-material. Hence I suggest that Moule's suggestion is not tenable.

G.B. Caird and William Barclay argue that 'the physical body is intimately, vitally, and indissolubly connected with the spiritual body.'[56] Both endorse St Paul's analogy of the plant growing out of the dead seed,[57] but overlook the fact that the two processes are in no way comparable because no plant ever grows out of a seed which has been totally dispersed or cremated, and because resurrection bodies are supposed not to grow slowly but to be resurrected at adulthood. Further, neither they nor any other contemporary exponent of real material continuity even attempts to spell out how this continuity might be worked out in practice — how the transformed body gets to heaven, where heaven is, or any other of the many difficulties I considered in Chapters 3 and 4. Hence I conclude that 're-embodiment in heaven' is popular today because it is the only understanding of resurrection of the body which still seems a possibility. Let us now spell out the full implications of this idea, and the concept of personhood which it entails.

The first implication of the thought that we will have bodies in heaven is that heaven must be a place — it must have spatial dimensions. As Austin Farrer points out, 'If heaven is completely non-spatial, then ... the heavenly life must be a featureless sea of feeling, a shapeless ecstasy; or anyhow, nothing you could fairly call the resurrection-state of man.'[58] I think Farrer under-estimates the possibilities for personal life in a purely mental existence, and I shall defend the worthwhileness of such a concept in a later chapter. But Farrer's main point seems utterly valid, that nothing one could call 'a resurrection state of a man' can be non-spatial. Bodies must live somewhere; this is entailed by being or having a body. *The Concise Oxford Dictionary*[59] reminds us that the word 'body' describes 'a material organism', 'a thing perceptible to the senses' possessing 'solidity, or substantial character'. The whole point of talking about 'resurrection of the body', rather than 'immortality of the soul', is that a bodiless, immaterial, intellectual, non-locatable soul is held by some writers to be inadequate for full personal existence. The resurrection of the body has been chosen by Christian writers in explicit contrast to the notion of an immortal soul, and if words mean anything, this explicit contrast must be thought of as indicating some real difference between the two concepts. This difference between the two notions is that a body is spatial and a soul is non-spatial.

Farrer is the only writer to have taken note of this point. Yet, with the exception of Wheeler Robinson,[60] all the writers in my sample affirm belief in the resurrection of the body, and go out of their way to deny the adequacy of the soul's immortality. Aldwinckle and Baker are not so emphatic as the others on this point, but even they say that our immortality must be in an embodied form.[61] Vidler says that 'the Christian hope is much more than survival as a disembodied spirit with all the vague unreality which that suggests';[62] A.M. Ramsey finds immortality 'distressingly dull, and missing the gift of the gospel';[63] Gore and Winter insist 'not the soul, but the person';[64] the Dutch Catechism says 'we cannot think of ourselves as an isolated 'I' disconnected from our body ... it is not biblical usage to speak of a purely disembodied soul of man';[65] Moss and Baillie insist that eternal life requires possession of a body;[66] and Hodgson writes 'The thought of a disembodied spirit suggests a pale, anaemic kind of existence, stripped of the powers of self-expression that in a healthy body make life worth living. It means something to say that life will not be less but more fully vigorous and active than anything we experience here.'[67]

In the light of this insistence that we must be re-embodied, it is astonishing to find that the question of the whereabouts of heaven is either totally ignored, or answered with the assertion that heaven has no location. Vidler describes 'the conditions of life after death as transcending the limitations of the space-time process.'[68] David Winter says 'spatial ideas are irrelevant to a place which is not "in" a space-time environment';[69] Archbishop Ramsey writes

> We warn ourselves against supposing that "the other world" is a thing or a place standing over against this one ... It is indeed true that for the Biblical writers and for much Christian thought in post-Biblical times, heaven ... was a place beyond the sky. Thither Christ had gone up at his ascension, and there the saints reigned with him in dazzling light. Yet within this language of locality, just because it was language about God, there was present something which strained it and turned it into the symbol of realities which transcended locality altogether; the supremacy of Christ everywhere, and the union of Christians with God through him ... The spatial conception of the "other world" lingered, but the heart of Christian belief knew from the beginning that it was using symbols for a God-Christ-mankind relationship beyond locality.[70]

The difficulty facing a Christian writer today is that modern discoveries about 'The Physical Basis of Personality',[71] and the findings of Old Testament Scholarship, have combined to make him feel that, in Paternoster's words, 'Resurrection of the Body is not only more biblical than Immortality of the Soul, it also makes better sense.'[72] At the same time however the cosmological discoveries of the 17th Century, and the subsequent gradual change in the meaning of the English word 'heaven', has caused heaven to be spiritualised into describing a state of being, rather than a future dwelling place. What writers have overlooked in the main is that these two movements of thought are mutually incompatible. An immortal soul can be thought of as existing without location in a non-located heaven. But a resurrected body requires to live somewhere. Therefore the child's question 'Where is heaven?' cannot be answered with the assertion that 'it's nowhere, it's a state of being', if one also wants to say that after death we are to be resurrected. This situation is not always obvious because people tend to deal with only one question at a time, and because writers tend to discuss heaven in a different chapter from the one in which they discuss resurrection so they do not notice that their answers are in fact mutually incompatible.

Farrer, however, does face up to this difficulty, perhaps because he is one of the few Christian thinkers to have noticed that the radical re-thinking of physics in the present century has provided a way in which the Christian thinker can postulate a location for heaven, as we saw in Chapter 4. It is thus quite possible that there may be a spatial heaven in which our personalities are to be re-embodied with quite different bodies. Hence the idea for which most modern Christian writers seem, despite their internal inconsistencies, to be arguing is in fact a possibility. What is ruled out however is any notion of the slightest material connection between the two bodies.

What doctrine of man is required by such a view of heaven? The point of contact between the two worlds cannot be physical; if therefore 'I' am to exist in the future in this heaven in another space, it follows that my 'personal identity' cannot be equated with my present body. Hence the concept of re-embodiment in heaven requires a concept of the soul as its necessary condition. Therefore I believe that the consensus of modern Christian thought is quite reasonable in its affirmations about the nature of the possible future life, but is wrong in its denials. It is right to affirm that we could get new and different bodies in heaven; that there would be no material continuity between our earthly and heavenly bodies; and that what ensures our personal continuity could be described in terms like 'the person', 'the essential part of what we are', 'the vital principal of our being', 'the pattern of what we are', and 'our moral and intellectual qualities'. But I have suggested that the consensus is wrong, because inconsistent, in denying that heaven is a place, and in denying the validity of describing what ensures our continuity as being a 'soul'; for in fact the descriptions I have given above of what they believe survives are the meanings the *Oxford Concise Dictionary* gives to the word 'soul', and it seems simply contradictory to deny the word 'soul' as unbiblical, and yet to affirm everything which the dictionary tells us that word means.

However, to show that rational belief in a future life depends upon the validity of the concept of the soul does nothing, in itself, to re-habilitate that concept. That is therefore a task to which we must now turn.

# Part III

# 6 A Defence of the Concept of the Soul

What is it that constitutes my personal identity? That is the major question facing any speculation about a possible future life. If my selfhood is necessarily dependent on bodily continuity, then there seems no sense in which my conscious personal self could exist after the cremation and scattering of my corpse. On the other hand if Descartes was right in arguing that 'This *I*, that is to say, the mind, by which I am what I am, is entirely distinct from the body',[1] then this fundamental objection to belief in life after death is removed. Let us therefore examine the arguments which led Descartes to this conclusion.

Descartes' ideas were the result of his search for an absolutely certain foundation upon which to build a philosophical system. Consequently he decided to reject 'everything in which I could suppose the slightest reason for doubt.' Accordingly he rejected knowledge derived from the senses 'because our senses sometimes play us false', and he rejected knowledge based on human reasoning

> because there are men who make mistakes in reasoning ... [and] I was as liable to error as anyone else ... And finally ... I resolved to pretend that nothing which had entered my mind was any more true than the illusions of my dreams. But immediately afterwards I became aware that, while I decided thus to think that everything was false, it followed necessarily that I who thought thus must be something; and observing that this truth: 'I think, therefore I am', was so certain and so evident that all the most extravagant suppositions of the

sceptics were not capable of shaking it, I judged that I could accept it without scruple as the first principle of the philosophy I was seeking.[2]

Descartes' point is that although as a hypothetical exercise one may attempt to doubt absolutely everything, the one thing that it is impossible for the doubter to doubt is the reality of his own doubting. But since only an existent being can doubt it follows that the doubter must exist, and that thinking must be of the essence of his identity.

This argument has been strongly criticised by A.J. Ayer[3] and Bertrand Russell for illegitimately using the word 'I'. According to Russell, Descartes ought to state his ultimate premise in the form 'there are thoughts'. The word 'I' is gramatically convenient, but does not describe a datum. When he goes on to say "I am a thing which thinks", he is already using uncritically the apparatus of categories handed down by scholasticism. He nowhere proves that thoughts need a thinker, nor is there any reason to believe this except in a grammatical sense.'[4]

This criticism is unfair for, as Copleston points out,

> Descartes was convinced . . . that after thinking away all that can be doubted I apprehend, not simply a thinking or a thought, which is uncritically attributed to a thinker as substance, but rather a thinking I or ego. I apprehend not merely a 'thinking' but 'me thinking'. He may be right or wrong in believing that he, or any other individual, does apprehend this immediately as an indubitable datum, but, he would not be in the position of assuming uncritically a doctrine of substance.[5]

The question is whether or not Descartes was right to suppose that his primary datum was 'me thinking', rather than 'there are thoughts.' At this point I side whole-heartedly with Descartes for I do not know what meaning to attach to the notion of an un-owned thought. Unless the doubting thoughts are mine I cannot see how I could apprehend them as data. I know that many distinguished philosophers including Hume,[6] Russell, Wittgenstein[7] and the young Ayer see no reason to believe that thoughts need a thinker, and it is a cardinal tenet of Theravada Buddhism that 'there is no thinker behind the thought' or indeed any subject of any experiencing:

> Mere suffering exists, but no sufferer is found;
> The deeds are, but no doer is found.[8]

But the notion that doing, suffering and thinking can be isolated from agents, sufferers and thinkers seems to me to be as impossible as the notion of a Cheshire cat vanishing and leaving only its grin behind. When Wittgenstein allegedly declared that in the expression 'I have a toothache . . . the "I" does not denote a possessor',[9] I can only comment that I wish he were right!

More recently Ayer has adopted a different approach to Descartes' *Cogito*. He now regards it as a valid argument but one that gives expression to an uninteresting and trivial point of logic: 'If I start with the fact that I am doubting, I can validly draw the conclusion that I think and that I exist. That is to say, if there is such a person as myself, then there is such a person as myself, and if I think, I think . . . His argument does not prove that he, or anyone, knows anything.'[10]

I suggest that Ayer reaches this conclusion by considering the *Cogito* in isolation from its context. Descartes is not concerned just to show that a thinking being must of necessity be an existent being. His aim is rather to show that my thinking is of the essence of my identity. It is the fact that I think that makes me 'me'. Descartes wants to show that my mind is in fact my 'substance', whereas my body is in a strict sense 'accidental' to me. He does this by showing that I can doubt that I possess a body, but cannot doubt that I doubt.

Descartes recognises that concerning the reality of our 'having a body, and that there are stars and an earth . . . we may have a moral assurance . . . which is such that, short of being foolish, no one can doubt their existence.' However, 'when it is a question of metaphysical certainty, one cannot deny that there are not sufficient grounds for being absolutely assured, when one observes that one can in the same way imagine, being asleep, that one has another body, and that one sees other stars and another earth, without there being anything of the sort.'[11] Moreover, 'I could pretend that I had no body and that there was no world or place that I was in, but I could not pretend that I did not exist, and that, on the contrary, from the very fact that I thought of doubting the truth of other things, it followed very evidently and very certainly that I existed . . . I thereby concluded that I was a substance, of which the whole essence or nature consists in thinking, and which in order to exist, needs no place and depends on no material thing'.[12]

The point of this argument is that I must identify myself with my mind since I can imagine myself owning and using another body. Consider Professor Kneale's example: 'If I found one morning on looking into the mirror that the face I proposed to shave was unfamiliar, I should indeed be very much surprised, but I could not say that it was not my face if at the same time I had to admit that I saw with its eyes, talked with its lips, and in general had what we may call inner perceptions of it.' We would come to this conclusion because 'although we distinguish the bodies of other men by their various appearances, each of us recognises his own in a quite different way, namely as something with which he perceives and acts.'[13]

Kneale does not conclude from this argument that therefore my selfhood is a 'mental substance which can claim the body as its own', but rather he suggests that personal identity 'for each man . . . is the presence of a certain pattern in his experiences which convinces him that they are connected with a particular body.'[14] But I suggest that such a hypothesis cannot meet the circumstances which Kneale has just described. One cannot at the same time 'stress the importance of the body schema in each man's notion of himself',[15] and also hold that I could still be 'I' though in an unfamiliar body. I suggest that it is not merely 'difficult to avoid'[16] the notion of a mental substance in such a case but it is unreasonable to do so. If it is logically possible for me to exist in another body then my personal identity is not to be identified with my body as an externally recognisable entity, but rather with my internal, self-aware consciousness or mind.

My argument started from considering the hypothetical

situation of my looking into the mirror and seeing an unfamiliar face. But does this way of describing it prejudge the issue? If the face seen is really unfamiliar is it right to continue to use the word 'I', for according to Professor Geach and Penelhum, mental continuity is not sufficient to justify the assumption of continued personal identity? Penelhum urges that 'A criterion of identity has to be part of a publicly usable set of conceptual devices'.[17] And Geach points out that in any legal dispute about a person's identity, reliable medical evidence about scars, old fractures or dental treatment would always be regarded as more conclusive than mere claims to remember certain events.[18]

Geach is probably right in supposing that this would be true of a judicial inquiry, but this does not affect the case I am considering. In this case the word 'I' refers to the subject of the conscious experience of looking into a mirror and seeing an unfamiliar face. The subject of this experience might well find that others refused to recognise him as Paul Badham with all the subsequent legal, professional, financial and personal consequences this would entail for him. But if that subject possessed, and experienced as his own the memory, self-awareness and consciousness which Paul Badham had up to that moment enjoyed, he could not himself doubt that he, in himself, was the same person, even if in the end he decided to forego the use of the name Paul Badham as involving too many complications. He could have no choice about regarding himself as the person he felt himself to be, for as Professor John Hick rightly asks: 'What would it be to doubt that one is the person one is conscious of being?'[19]

Hence I think Descartes was right to say that 'I do not observe that any other thing necessarily belongs to my nature or essence except that I am a thinking thing, I rightly conclude that my essence consists in this alone ... and although I have a body to which I am very closely united, nevertheless .. it is certain that I, that is to say my mind, by which I am what I am, is entirely and truly distinct from it.'[20]

But is Descartes consistent in saying that the mind is distinct from the body and yet closely united to it? I suggest that he is simply being faithful to the facts of human experience. On the one hand there is ample evidence to support his view that the physical workings of the 'bodily machine' can be explained by solely natural causes.[21] On the other hand it is equally a part of our daily experience that minds and bodies do affect one another. Clearly there is a tension between these two facets of our experience. That is why the mind-body relation has always been regarded as one of the 'problems' of philosophy. I suggest however that Descartes' theory of a logical distinction between the categories of mind and body, coupled with his insistence on the reality of a two-way interaction between them, may be the hypothesis which does most justice to empirical observation.

My defence of Cartesianism is very much at odds with most current writing on the philosophy of mind. It will therefore be necessary to devote the next two chapters to criticism of the increasingly popular alternative which is the theory of Mind/Brain Identity. However one reason why philosophers of mind have moved away from Cartesianism is that they were impressed by the arguments of Gilbert Ryle's *Concept of Mind*. Flew speaks for many when he says 'We have — thanks to Ryle — emancipated ourselves from the beguiling errors of Descartes.'[22] It therefore seems advisable for me to say why I believe that Ryle's critique fails. I shall be brief because I feel that a death-blow has been given to Ryle's argument by its detailed and systematic refutation in H.D. Lewis' work, *The Elusive Mind*.

Ryle assumes that Cartesianism implies an unreal disjunction between thought and action,[23] and that it entails solipsism.[24] He has little difficulty in showing the absurdity of such positions, but his argument is weakened by the fact that such beliefs form no part of what dualists actually, or necessarily, believe.[25] He assumes that the question, 'what is thought?' can be considered as equivalent to the question, 'how do I become aware of the presence of intelligence in others?' Consequently he regards mental activity as equivalent to the exercise of behavioural dispositions and skills and asserts that 'overt intelligent performances are not clues to the working of minds; they are those workings.'[26] The difficulty of this position is that it fails to do justice to the fact that very often, for example under totalitarian regimes, outward conformity does not imply inward assent, and it does not answer the question with which Cartesianism is concerned which is 'what is the nature of my own rational thinking?'

I believe that Lewis succeeds in showing that Descartes' position does not derive from a category mistake,[27] nor from the belief that bodies and minds can be said to exist in different senses.[28] Descartes' actual starting point is his attempt to give a positive account of what it is to think and consequently his argument is unaffected by Ryle's criticism.

I conclude therefore that Lewis succeeds in his task of refuting Ryle's arguments and hence removes some of the most commonly held intellectual barriers against contemporary acceptance of Cartesian dualism. But there are still difficulties. It seems increasingly hard to suppose that the soul is a special, divine creation inserted into the developing human embryo. However, although Descartes himself believed this,[29] I see no reason why a contemporary Cartesian should not say with John Hick that 'the soul is a divine creation in the same sense as the body — namely through the instrumentality of the entire evolution of the universe and within this of the development of life on our planet. Distinctive human mentality and spirituality emerges, in accordance with the divine purpose, in complex bodily organisms. But once it has emerged it is the vehicle, according to Christian faith, of a continuing creative activity only the beginnings of which have so far taken place.'[30]

Such a hypothesis is not new to the history of Christian thought for it can claim ancestry in the doctrine of 'Traducianism' defined in the *Oxford Dictionary of the Christian Church* as: 'The theory according to which the human soul is transmitted by the parents to the children.'[31] This was taught by Gregory of Nyssa and was the theory of the soul's origin to which St Augustine on the whole leaned. For although he had some hesitations about it, and at times favoured a theory of special creation or even of pre-existence, it was Traducianism which he most consistently taught.[32]

Although this doctrine fell into disfavour in the Middle

Ages I suggest that its re-habilitation is essential in our day. John Hick has stated that 'whilst it cannot be proved that the two factors of heredity and environment between them account for the entire range of the individual's character traits, it certainly seems that they do and that there is no need to postulate in addition the influence of a soul ... carrying basic dispositional characteristics ... supplied directly by God.'[33] In the light of this, the notion of a specially created soul seems a wholly unjustifiable concept but a Traducianist doctrine accords fully with what we know about the influence of both heredity and environment.

If this hypothesis is accepted, then the one major objection to Cartesianism that still remains is one already foreseen by Descartes himself. At one point Descartes confessed: 'I do not yet know whether ... the thinking nature which is in me ... is different from the corporeal nature to me, or whether both are merely one and the same thing.'[34] In this Descartes recognises that though mind and body are logically distinct this does not prove that therefore they must be contingently distinct. This challenge has re-emerged in recent years and we must therefore now turn our attention to it.

# 7 A Critique of the Mind-Brain Identity Theory

The Mind/Brain Identity Theory,[1] otherwise known as Central State Materialism, is, I believe, the main challenger to any dualist theory of man. Unlike behaviourism or epiphenomenalism, the Identity theory takes seriously the view that mental states can be causally effective. The upholder of the Identity theory will agree with the Cartesian dualist in the view that to describe a man as intelligent is not simply to say that he is apt to turn in an intelligent performance, it is also to say that an inner structure or condition of the man is an indispensable immediate causal factor in producing the intelligent performance. 'Intelligence' names not the performance pattern but one part of its cause, the inner and therefore mental part. Both the Cartesian and the Identity theorist believe that mental acts such as choosing, deciding or purposing are causally effective; both believe that mental states such as anxiety, hope, confidence or despair do not just describe anxious, hopeful, confident or despairing behaviour, but actually bring about that behaviour. Further, both the Cartesian and Identity theorist can agree that our mental qualities — our capacities of memory, thought, imagination and will — may be the prime characteristics of our personal identity, largely determining our character dispositions and self-awareness.

Both the Cartesian and the Identity theorist can agree on the importance of mind and may identify a person with his mind. Both may use dualist language to describe the influence of the mind on the body; body being the external, visible frame in which we now live and mind being the inner, motivating self. The difference lies on the answer to the empirical question 'what is the mind?' Briefly, the Cartesian identifies the mind with what we may call the soul — an immaterial, spiritual, non-locatable reality which uses the brain as its instrument of thought, while the Identity theorist identifies the mind with the brain — the central nervous system of the body.

In everyday life the Cartesian and the Central State Materialist will share the same experiences, and make judgements in the same way. Both will accept Feigl's assessment that 'Scientifically, the most plausible view to date is that there is a one-one (or at least a one-many) correspondence of mental states to neurophysiological process patterns.'[2] Both may accept that memories are stored chemically in our brains,[3] that the mechanism of thinking is to be explained by the way the nerve cells of the brain work together,[4] that whether our imagination is visual or conceptual depends on the nature of the brain's electrical system,[5] and that our genetic inheritance[6] and our hormonal structure[7] will profoundly shape our personality. The Identity theorist will see these facts as showing that 'What we call our minds is simply a way of talking about our brains' (Francis Crick)[8]. The Cartesian will see these facts as proving the truth of interactionism, namely that any change in our bodily state will have an effect upon our minds, and that any mental changes will have a simultaneous effect upon our brains. In short, changes in brain states will be recognised as necessitating mental changes whether we believe that the mind is the brain, or whether we believe that the brain is the instrument which the mind uses to think with in its present embodied state.

The difference between the two positions seems to be, as we shall argue below, that the Cartesian is able to take into account the data provided by psychical research, and that he can accept the Augustinian-Franciscan[9]— Eastern Orthodox[10] view that in mystical experience 'God is most truly present to the very soul and immediately knowable' (St Bonaventura).[11] Further, as I shall argue in the next chapter, a Cartesian can put forward a more satisfactory theory of knowledge and do better justice to the experienced freedom of the will. More crucial for my present thesis, a Cartesian can believe that it is not only logically, but also contingently, possible that the mind may survive the dissolution of the brain and either pass to a purely mental existence, or be clothed or equipped with a new body. The Identity theorist by contrast must, I believe, deny the alleged findings of psychical research, must reject the notion of immediate knowledge of God, and must hold that it has been discovered to be contingently impossible for the mind to survive the brain since, according to his theory, neuro-physiological research will show mind and brain to be one entity. Therefore despite the wide area of agreement noted between the two theories earlier, and despite the fact that in everyday life theorists of both schools will share the same attitudes and expectations, there remain important questions on which they fundamentally differ.

The identity between mind and brain which is postulated by the Identity theory is an identity of reality, not an identity of meaning or of the way in which we experience reality. The nature of this identity can be illuminated by considering U.T. Place's analogy of the discovered identity of clouds with 'water droplets, or other particles in sus-pension.'[12] Linguistically speaking there is a very great difference between what we mean by the word 'cloud' and by the phrase 'a mass of water-droplets in suspension.' Clouds for instance can be described as "fleecy", "downy", or 'like puffs of cotton wool', or 'like a transparent veil'.[13] Clouds can be thought of in religious mythology as means of transportation; thus Psalm 18 pictures God coming down from heaven with a dark cloud under his feet, and Jesus describes the Son of Man 'Coming on the clouds of heaven'.[14] Clouds can also be thought of as particularly daunting mountains, as in the reference to the King of Babylon climbing up the thunderclouds (Isaiah 14). Again, clouds can be thought of as symbols of divine glory, as in the Old Testament usage or as in the accounts of the trans-figuration.[15] In none of these cases would it make sense to substitute the phrase 'a mass of water-droplets in suspension.' The difference between clouds and water-droplets also extends to the ways we experience the two. When we are close enough to observe that the cloud is composed of water droplets, our experiences then are so different from those we enjoyed when observing the cloud that we use other words to describe these experiences: 'That which is a cloud when we observe it at a distance becomes a mist or fog when we are enveloped by it.'[16]

This analogy can help us to see that just as the difference between observing a fleecy cloud, and being enveloped in a mass of water-droplets does not rule out cloud/water-droplets identity, so the difference between having a mental experience and observing a brain-process does not preclude mind/brain identity.

The limitation of the analogy sketched above is that both clouds and water-droplets are recognised as such by the same methods. At a distance our visual senses tell us something is a cloud, as we move closer these same visual senses tell us that this cloud in fact consists of water-droplets. In the case of brain-processes and consciousness there is no such continuity between the two sets of observations involved. We need therefore to find another analogy to help us see that the existence of different methods of verification does not itself preclude the actual identity of two phenomena. In both language and experience 'lightning' is different from 'a motion of electrical charges.'[17] We observe the presence of lightning by our visual senses; we need instruments and knowledge to detect the presence of electrical charges. Nevertheless we do identify the two phenomena because whenever we observe lightning we can detect the presence of electrical charge, and because when we ourselves transmit electrical charges through the atmosphere we bring about on a smaller scale the same type of flash. It is possible of course to argue for an interacting dualism here, namely that the evidence only points to electrical charges always giving rise to lightning flashes when transmitted through the atmosphere, and for lightning flashes always giving rise to electrical charges. But here the dualism can be rightly disposed of by Occam's razor because nothing whatever is gained by postulating an interacting dualism. All the facts can be explained by a simple identification of the two phenomena. In such a situation the postulation of two entities is unnecessary, and is therefore to be rejected.

The case for the Mind/Brain Identity theory is that although talk of mental events has a quite different meaning from talk of brain processes, and although the former is experienced by introspection and the latter by observation, nevertheless their inseparable concomitance makes it reasonable to apply Occam's razor and assert their identity. As J.J.C. Smart argues, 'If the brain-process theory and dualism are equally consistent with the facts, then the principles of parsimony and simplicity seem to be to decide overwhelmingly in favour of the brain-process theory.'[18] I accept this argument. My case is that the Mind/Brain Identity theory and dualism are not equally consistent with the facts.

This may seem a bold claim to make in the light of the assertion made by Identity theorists that 'At present the drift of scientific thought is clearly set towards the physicochemical hypothesis. And we have nothing better to go on' (D.M. Armstrong).[19] This is certainly the view of some of the most eminent scientists of our time. Francis Crick, Nobel Prize winner of 1962, writes 'To those of you who may be vitalists,[20] I make this prophecy: what everyone believed yesterday, and you believe today, only cranks will believe tomorrow.'[21] Jacques Monod, Nobel Prize winner of 1965, is of a like mind[22] and, on a humbler level, such views seem taken for granted by my contemporaries working in scientific faculties.

Nevertheless when one turns from scientists in general, and geneticists in particular, to those working in the relevant field of neuro-physiological research, the situation seems, to an outsider, to be rather different. Ian Barbour notes 'Mind-brain dualism has been adopted by many prominent-physiologists. In a British symposium all the scientists agreed that the neural activity of the brain somehow interacts with the private world of the mind.'[23] This statement refers to the contributions made by Sherrington, Adrian, Clark, Brain and Penfield to the symposium edited by P. Laslett, *The Physical Basis of Mind.* This was published in 1950, but the same judgement could be made concerning the twenty-two leading neuro-physiologists who contributed to the symposium *The Brain and Conscious Experience* in 1966.[24] In his preface to this symposium Sir John Eccles writes 'Though we differ widely in our philosophical beliefs, each of us I think would regard the theme of this symposium as raising challenging and fundamental scientific problems. We would not range ourselves with those obscurantist philosophers who classify problems relating to mind and brain as pseudo-problems arising from so-called category mistakes.'[25] Wilder Penfield, President of the College of Physicians and Surgeons of Canada and described by Professor A. Gomes[26] as the greatest authority in the world on the brain, writes in this symposium 'It is hard for us to conceive two separate elements but it is equally incomprehensible that there should only be one element presenting itself as two.'[27]

Sir John Eccles who gained the Nobel Prize in 1963 for his experimental work on the brain is even more insistent on the importance of dualism in his book *Facing Reality* (published in 1970).[28] He asserts that those who hold 'the materialistic or mechanistic philosophy . . . display a complete misunderstanding of the working of the brain.'[29] He criticises the Identity theory on the ground that 'This extraordinary belief cannot be accommodated to the fact that only a minute amount of cortical activity finds expression in conscious experience. Contrary to this physicalist creed, I believe that the prime reality of my experiencing self cannot with propriety be identified with some aspects of its experiences and imaginings — such as brains and neurones and nerve impulses and even complex spatio-temporal patterns of impulses.'[30]

Eccles, happily picking up Ryle's critical terminology, insists that the brain is just the sort of machine a ghost could operate.[31] Wilder Penfield believes that the brain can profitably be compared to some kind of exceedingly complex computer, and with this similarity too, that like any other computer it needs an operator. He asks: 'Can we visualize a spiritual element . . . capable of controlling this mechanism? When a patient is asked about the movement which he carries out as a result of cortical stimulation, he is never in any doubt about it. He knows that there is a difference between automatic action and voluntary action. He would agree that something else finds its dwelling place between the sensory complex and the motor mechanism, that there is a switchboard operator as well as a switchboard.[32]

This is not the place for a non-specialist to discuss the pros and cons of complex scientific discussions. It may be, as Crick implies, that the reason why 'vitalistic ideas . . . are held by some of the leading workers in this field' is that the study of the nervous system is 'relatively speaking a scientifically backward area of study.'[33] Where men of the stature of Francis Crick and Jacques Monod on the one side, and John Eccles and Wilder Penfield on the other, show such radical divergence of views the only conclusion an outsider can validly come to is that the situation is fluid. When, therefore, Identity theorists assert that the future development of neuro-physiology will establish their position they are making, as Smart admits, 'a confession of faith.'[34] It is at least possible that conventional neuro-physiological inquiry may come to a quite different conclusion.

The conclusion which seems most likely, however, is that the interpretation of neuro-physiological data will remain permanently ambiguous, because almost any conceivable findings could be interpreted as illustrating mind/brain interaction, just as well as being interpreted as showing mind/brain identity. I say almost any findings, because it does seem possible that further experimentation in splitting the two hemispheres of the brain apart and observing consequential effects upon the unity of conscious experience might possibly establish the truth of the identity thesis. If it could be established that each half of a divided brain possessed its own consciousness, then I would regard dualism as disproved. I accept that it would be logically possible to argue that even this could be explained in interactionist terms as showing that division of the brain causes division of the mind, but I would myself reach for Occam's razor to excise so vacuous a concept as a mind capable of becoming two minds as a result of brain division.

The results of present research on brain division are clearly ambiguous since Crick[35] and Eccles[36] both use the findings to support their mutually contradictory positions. Professor Bremer states: 'None of the surgeries aiming at the disruption of hemispheric synergy has been found capable of altering seriously the mental unity of man.'[37] All such experiments 'were without any overt influence on their volitional conduct.' Sperry's experiments showed that in no case did they 'experience any splitting of their mental unity'.[38] On the other hand the dominant hemisphere controls all the speech mechanisms and therefore only this hemisphere can communicate its experiences to us. If the minor hemisphere were independently conscious we could not know, because it could not communicate its consciousness to us. This is a serious difficulty because when the two split hemispheres are prevented from communicating with each other each hemisphere can separately be trained to perform actions which show 'perception, cognition, volition, learning and memory.'[39] It is possible therefore that each hemisphere may have an independent mental life, but against this Eccles argues that 'All the evidence produced by these nine cases is explicable by the postulate that, when bereft of commisural linkages with the dominant hemisphere, the minor hemisphere behaves as a computer with inbuilt skills of movement, with recognition of form and function of objects and with the ability to learn.'[40] Eccles holds that the experiments prove that after the brain is split 'the conscious self, with all its linguistic and sophisticated behavioural performance, seems to be represented solely in the dominant hemisphere ... Unity of conscious experience is maintained at the expense of a loss of all the activities of the minor hemisphere.'[41] In his view the minor hemisphere functions as an unconscious computer reacting to stimuli. By contrast Crick supposes both hemispheres to be conscious, but that there is no way the minor hemispheres can communicate its experience to us.[42] R.W. Sperry does put forward some evidence which suggests that the minor hemisphere may have a will of its own, since it does control the left hand and arm, and he describes how one patient spoke of his own 'sinister left hand pushing his wife away while his right hand had wanted to help her with something.'[43] Sperry hopes that at some later date it might be possible 'by more devious pathways' to connect up the minor hemisphere to the dominant hemisphere and so 'enable it to achieve linguistic expression.'[44] It is possible therefore that in the future the Identity theory may be scientifically established by sophisticated experiments on split-brained patients.

   I would however be surprised to read about such experiments having been successful, because I believe there is already a considerable body of empirical facts which are incompatible with the Identity hypothesis. I refer to the data of psychical research. My contention is that telepathy is an empirical fact and that telepathy is incompatible with the Identity theory. Both assertions are highly controversial; so let us discuss the evidence for each.

Francis Crick dismisses any kind of extra-sensory perception with contempt.

> The most striking thing about the work of the last thirty years on ESP has been its complete failure to produce any technique whatsoever which is scientifically acceptable. There is no known way, by a special screening procedure, by the use of drugs, or by any other method, to discover people who can communicate in this way, and be proved to sceptical observers to do so. No one truly reproducible experiment has been devised although the record is thick with fakes and sloppy experimentation. We must conclude either that the phenomenon does not exist, or that it is too difficult to study by present methods, or that the people who work on these problems are hopelessly third rate. ESP has all the appearance of a completely void science like astrology, in which no genuine experiments exist, and the only 'results' are due to bad experimentation or to faking, either by subject or experimenter, conscious or unconscious.[45]

This is the considered opinion of the man responsible for what Monod describes as 'without any doubt the most important discoveries ever made in biology.'[46] Yet is Crick's judgement in any sense fair or accurate? Does even Crick have the right to describe as 'hopelessly third rate' 'the steadily growing and impressive list of Nobel Laureates in physics and medicine, professors of philosophy, fellows of the Royal Society, and the Soviet Academy of Science' who regard ESP as a 'potentially important area of investigation?'[47] One cannot help remembering Crick's dismissal of neuro-physiology as 'a relatively backward area of study'[48] and noting his misuse of the term 'vitalist' to describe any dualist theory. Professor Eysenck's judgement seems appropriate: 'Scientists, especially when they leave the particular field in which they have specialised, are just as ordinary, pig-headed and unreasonable as anybody else, and their unusually high intelligence only makes their prejudices all the more dangerous.'[49]

A fairer assessment of the intellectual validity of telepathy might be that of Professor Eysenck in 1960: 'Unless there is a gigantic conspiracy involving some thirty University departments all over the world, and several hundred highly respected scientists in various fields, many of them originally hostile to the claims of the psychical researchers, the only conclusion the unbiased observer can come to must be that there does exist a small body of people who obtain knowledge existing in other people's minds or in the outer world, by means as yet unknown to science.'[50] Arthur Koestler comments on Eysenck's statement: 'The above was written in 1960. In the decade that has passed since, the situation has changed ... Instead of some thirty University departments ... there is now hardly a country in the world which does not have one or several university departments engaged in para-psychological research — with Russia leading the field; and the hypothesis of a gigantic conspiracy would have to involve not several hundred but thousands of respectable scientists.'[51]

The most impressive evidence for telepathy comes from two sources; Professor Rhine's work at the Para-psychology Institute at Duke University,[52] and Professor Vasiliev's work at the Leningrad Institute for Brain Research.[53] Rhine's method was basically through card guessing.[54] He used specially constructed Zener cards, which had only five markings. The sender turned up card after card, each one screened from view, and a receiver tried telepathically to guess which of the Zener cards were turned up. The probability of a correct 'hit' by pure chance was therefore one in five, or 20 per cent. In 1934 Rhine published the complete record of 85,000 card calling tries and the average of successful calls turned out to be 28 per cent not 20 per cent.[55] To a non-mathematician this may seem to be a trivial result, but the chances against this occurring fortuitously are astronomical. According to the universally accepted probability calculus a deviation of 8 per cent from chance in this number of guesses is virtually impossible to account for. The same sort of success was experienced by two English experimenters Thouless and Soal. Koestler comments 'The statistical results obtained in the experiments by Rhine, Soal, Thouless, and so on, constitute the strongest evidence to confound the sceptical scientist.[56] ... This is what has convinced so many sceptics, particularly physicists, that ESP is a hard reality.[57] But there remain questions about this method of considering ESP, and there are doubts about the accuracy of the results. C.E.M. Hansel has examined the best experiments made and he has pointed to opportunities for conscious or unconscious cheating in every one of them.[58] He has further pointed out that many experimenters in other universities have failed to obtain chances better than normal, and that no one today seems to obtain results as good as those claimed in the thirties. Tom Paine's question sums up Hansel's viewpoint, 'Is it more probable that nature should go out of course or that a man should tell a lie?'[59] The question has its force to any one who is completely sure that he knows what nature's course is. The Cardinal did not need to look down Galileo's telescope; he knew there were and could be no such thing as sun spots and therefore Galileo was lying when he claimed to see them. The case against Hansel is the sheer unlikelihood that the hundreds of eminent researchers into ESP could all have faked their results. As Dr J. Beloff puts it, 'Those now implicated in telepathy include a sizeable number of disinterested people of the highest academic and professional standing. The suggestion that such persons have deliberately sacrificed their integrity, and risked ruining their reputation for no other reason than to perpetuate a puerile hoax must surely strike one as impertinent.'[60] As we noted earlier, the number of eminent persons and societies now involved in telepathic experiments seems increasingly to make the fraud hypothesis less and less credible. In 1969 the American Association for the Advancement of Science finally accepted the application of the Para-psychological Association to become an affiliated body.[61] In February 1971 the American National Aeronautics and Space Administration arranged that during his moon mission Colonel

Mitchell should establish telepathic contact with four selected subjects on earth following Rhine's classic card-guessing experiments. The results have not yet been published, but according to initial reports they 'Far exceeded anything expected.'[62]

A quite different method was employed at the Leningrad Institute for Brain Research by Professor Lenoid Vasiliev. The normal difficulty of transmitting messages telepathically from one person to another is the difficulty of establishing initial contact. Vasiliev circumnavigated this difficulty by first establishing control over the recipient of the messages by hypnosis and then sending messages by telepathy which were instantly obeyed. In one report of his work, published in English under the title *Experiments in Mental Suggestion*, Vasiliev records several series of experiments in which hypnotized subjects were sent to sleep and awakened at a distance, and at will. On occasion the distance was as great as from Leningrad to Sevastopol. One interesting development was that placing both sender and recipient in Faraday cages had no effect on the success of the communication. I will return to this point later, mentioning now only Vasiliev's comment that it 'was contrary to all our predictions, an unforeseen and confusing discovery.'[63] This bewilderment came about because Vasiliev's aim was not to prove simply that telepathy happened, but that it happened through some form of mental radio. His results however proved the reality of telepathy but disproved the possibility that mental radio could explain it. Koestler mentions that the experiments recorded in this book have been followed by many others in which telepathic communication between towns as distant as Moscow and Leningrad has been carried out en masse with thousands of subjects.[64] These experiments have resulted in a flood of subsequent Soviet experiments in telepathy. In 1958 there were two scientific publications on para-psychology in Russia, in 1967 there were thirty-five, and in 1969 there were seventy. Meanwhile publications against parapsychology have gone up only from one in 1958 to four in 1969. Vasiliev's conclusion, which he attributes to an eminent Soviet rocket pioneer, is that 'The phenomena of telepathy can no longer be called into question.'[65]

The great advantage of Vasiliev's work is summed up by Keith Campbell: 'Not even Hansel, that most ingenious deviser of ruses, can fault the experimental methods used.'[66] My conclusion therefore is that there is now sufficient evidence from many different sources to make it reasonable to accept the conclusions of the American NASA and of the Soviet Academy of Sciences that telepathy is a reality.[67]

But does accepting telepathy rule out a materialist theory of mind? That is the second question we must investigate. My case is that it does, but I am conscious that in holding this view I am parting company with those whose judgement has led me to accept telepathy as a reality — Vasiliev and Eysenck. Vasiliev strongly dissociates himself with those who use telepathy as a bulwark for outmoded mentalist ideas. He is quite confident that ultimately a satisfactory physical theory will be found. 'The problem resolves itself into the search for a form of energy the properties of which are as yet unknown and specific to substances of such advanced nature as the human brain.'[68] Eysenck, after the judgement I have already cited that acceptance of telepathy was 'the only conclusion the unbiased can come to', warns 'This should not be interpreted as giving any support to such notions as survival after death, philosophical idealism or anything else.'[69]

But the problems which telepathy raises for the Identity theory cannot be brushed aside by the expression of the hope that in the future a new form of energy may be found, or by the apparent belief that we can accept telepathy without it affecting the rest of our thinking. I believe that Feigl, Keith Campbell, and D.M. Armstrong are more realistic in seeing that the acceptance of telepathy would seriously weaken the materialist case. Herbert Feigl believes that 'it is conceivable that the "facts" of para-psychology will require emergentist or even interactionist explanations.'[70] D.M. Armstrong regards psychical research as 'the small black cloud on the horizon of a materialist theory of mind'[71] and Keith Campbell spells out in careful detail precisely why this is so:

Parapsychological phenomena, by definition, demonstrate capacities of mind which exceed any capacities of brain.

The brain is receptive only to information which arrives by neural pathways, and so is confined to perception by way of the senses. If some people can learn more about distant, hidden, or future fact than memory and inference from sense perception can teach them, then their minds are just not brains ... The brain is capable of receiving information about the mind of another but only by perception of the other's body, bodily acts, effects of such bodily acts and perception of reports from yet other people. If some minds are receptive to the contents of the mind of another by some more direct means such as telepathy then those minds are just not brains ... if even a single example of para-normal phenomena is genuine, Central State Materialism is false.[72]

It is of course true that the para-normal powers displayed in telepathy might be accommodated in a new, expanded physical science. Television, for instance, is para-normal with respect to Newton's physics but not to ours. In the same way, telepathy is para-normal with respect to today's science, but might not be so to the science of the next century. Hans Berger, the physiologist who discovered the technique of recording brain-waves with the electro-encephalograph, has suggested for example that the 'psychic energy' involved in telepathy might turn out to be 'a form of physical energy, interchangeable with other forms.'[73] The acceptance of this hypothesis would, Berger claims, enable us to give a physicalist explanation of telepathy. According to Berger, in telepathy 'electrical energy is transformed into "psychic energy", which can be diffused to any distance, passing through obstacles without attenuation; that on reaching the subject's brain it is there transformed back into electrical energy, thereby producing neural patterns and experiences corresponding to those of the agent.'[74]

It seems to me that Berger is simply saying that the discovery of a radically new form of physical energy, namely 'psychic energy', might enable physicists of the future to accommodate telepathy within their world view. I agree with Keith Campbell's comments on this issue: 'The fact that some neo-materialism might survive the establishment of para-normal truths would not vindicate Central-State Materialism. For Central-State Materialism is a materialism based on our present physical and chemical science. If that science is inadequate, the materialism based on it is false.'[75] In other words, the Mind-Brain Identity theory states that mental events are to be explained solely in terms of events in the central nervous system, and the reasoning behind this hypothesis depends entirely upon the validity of contemporary assumptions about the nature of material reality. At present those who advocate materialism assume the continuance of our present materialism. D.M. Armstrong writes 'At present the drift of scientific thought is clearly set towards the physico-chemical view of man and we have nothing better to go on ... this is not to say that in the future new evidence and new problems may not come to light which will force science to reconsider the physico-chemical view of man.'[76] Armstrong accepts the argument that it would be very difficult to see how telepathy could be reconciled to Identity by some future new developments. He speculates 'Could there not be as yet undiscovered physical processes which link one central nervous system with another, and so permit the transmission of information?' He thinks this may be so but is very doubtful for 'if we consider the particular nature of the alleged phenomena, then, if they actually occur, it is not easy to find explanations within the framework of physics as we know it.'[77] He thinks that the suggestion that telepathic communication 'is mediated by some physical radiation emitted by one central nervous system and picked up by another' was an initially promising one but notes that Vasiliev's experiments with Faraday cages disprove it. He asks despairingly 'what other channels of physical communication between subject and object can be suggested?' We could say that the radiation involved is quite unlike the physical radiation blocked by 'radiation-proof boxes. But then we are beginning to abandon the known structure of physics.' 'It is not at all easy to see how these special powers could be reconciled with the present conceptions of physics ... the consideration of psychical research must introduce a note of caution into the use of "argument from physics" for it raises a real doubt whether physics is supreme.'[78]

These arguments help one to understand Vasiliev's distress when he disproved the mental radio theory he was commissioned to verify. 'The result was contrary to all our predictions, an unforeseen and confusing discovery',[79] for the exclusion of telepathy taking the form of radiation spoilt the one hypothesis which might have contained telepathy within a physicalist world view.

Adrian Dobbs suggests that telepathy is brought about by particles of imaginary mass interacting with particles of real mass. The advantage of this theory is that these imaginary particles would be undetectable by any radiation screen and could travel any distance.[80] This suggestion owes its existence to the mathematically useful concepts of imaginary numbers, and virtual particles, but to treat such entities as having reality outside the calculus in which they have their rightful place seems to me to involve a misuse of terms. Y.P. Terleisky, from whose work Dobbs draws the concept, is careful to point out that although 'Particles with imaginary mass are not forbidden categorically as if they were physically unreal', what is forbidden 'is the process in which the emission of such particles . . . is associated with an increase of entropy of the radiatior.' 'The emission or absorption of such particles takes place . . . without a change in the entropy of the radiator or receiver.'[81] In other words, although the particles certainly possess a reality within the logistic calculus in which they are useful concepts, it is quite wrong to attribute causal efficacy to them. If they cannot cause change in the entropy of either radiatior or receiver, they cannot possess even enough energy to bring about the microscopic changes involved in the firing of a single neurone. If particles of imaginary mass are incapable of any influence they cannot even produce the 'small' undetectable influence required to bring about a minute change in brain state which would be sufficient by chain-reaction to set off enough neurones to produce an overt piece of behaviour. In other words Dobbs cannot use the imaginary particles of Terleisky, which are capable of no influence, to bring about the minute brain changes which Eccles states require only 'small influence.'[82]

Professor C.W.K. Mundle has drawn attention to a

revolutionary physicalist theory put forward by Ninian Marshall who

> suggests that in telepathy the state of the agent's brain affects that of the subject, without there being any continuous chain of intervening events or indeed any transmission of energy. To render this intelligible, he offers his 'Hypothesis of Resonance', which states 'that any two substances exert an influence on each other which tends to make them become more alike, the strength of this influence increases with the product of their complexities, and decreases with the difference between their patterns'. This hypothetical force he labels 'the Eidopoic Influence'. He argues that this influence has hitherto produced observable effects only in the form of ESP, because the human brain is by far the most complex structure in the world, but he predicts that telepathic interaction will be detectable between computing machines if or when these can be made sufficiently complex in structure.[83]

The objection to this theory is, as Mundle rightly says, that one cannot describe as a physical force something which involves no energy transfer because 'for physicists, physical transactions involve, by definition, a transfer of energy.'[84]

My conclusion therefore is that telepathy is incompatible with the physico-chemical doctrine of mind put forward by identity theorists, and since this physico-chemical doctrine is tied up with our understanding of what the laws of physics and chemistry are, a fundamental change in our understanding of such laws would remove the foundations on which the Identity theory is built.

Thus I believe that the data provided by telepathy disprove the Identity theory. I believe that Identity theorists have an urgent duty to face up to the new facts now available. It will not do for Feigl to say 'As an empiricist I must at least go through the motions of an "open mind" in these regards.'[85] Going through the motions is not enough! Likewise, Armstrong should not simply say 'The Central State Materialist has an intellectual duty to consider very carefully the alleged results of psychical research.'[86] He should show in his work that he takes his own words seriously. Two or three pages out of three hundred and seventy, and complete misunderstanding of Vasiliev, is not very careful consideration. (Vasiliev's experiments involve commands by telepathy to hypnotised subjects. Armstrong supposes that they involved guesses made about what was going on in other people's minds[87] — as if Vasiliev were a pupil of Rhine!) Campbell's position I find odd. He cites the card-guessing type of experiment, and then alludes to Hansel's criticism of it. He then notes than not even Hansel can fault Vasiliev's method,[88] but then he proceeds to repeat Hansel's dismissal of para-psychological data without noting that on his own judgement Vasiliev's experiments cannot thus be faulted. Hence I believe that although both Campbell and Armstrong are aware of the existence of Vasiliev's work both avoid facing up to it.

Earlier I stated that my position was that if the brain-process theory and dualism were equally consistent with the facts then I would favour the former on grounds of parsimony, but I stated that my case was that they were not both equally consistent with the facts since only dualism could account for the data of psychical research and mystical experience. I have now presented my reason for believing in the reality of telepathy and its incompatibility with the Identity theory; but what of mystical experience? I consider mystical experience to be experientially much more important than telepathy, in so far as many more people enjoy religious experiences of one kind or another than experience telepathy. Mystical experience is, if genuine, only compatible with dualism. Lossky describes the experience thus: 'The divine light being given in mystical experience surpasses at the same time both sense and intellect. It is immaterial and is not apprehended by the senses.'[89] He notes that all the greatest theologians of the Eastern Orthodox tradition insist on the immediacy of the mystic's knowledge of God and that it is neither mediated nor assisted by the senses.[90] A similar approach may be seen in what Tillich calls the 'Augustinian solution'[91] to the philosophy of religion. In this Augustinian-Franciscan approach it is asserted that 'God is knowable in himself without media.' St Bonaventura says 'God is most truly present to the soul and immediately knowable.'[92]

This type of religious understanding depends upon a dualist understanding of man, for it asserts that God can make his reality, his presence, known to us other than through neural pathways. In other words that our knowledge of God can be understood as communicated to us through some process akin to telepathy, direct to the mind, not via sensory stimuli and brain process. My own belief is that this type of religious experience is at the root of most people's deepest religious feeling, and that the Thomist way of moving from the world to God represents a second reflective stage in the person's religious development. Of course much religious experience takes the form of considering the beauty of the world or of worship or of a sense of duty, and abstracting from these experiences to the notion of a transcendent God, but I suggest that this movement from the world to the transcendent depends upon a pre-existing, mystical-intuitive, immediate awareness of God, which can only be a reality if dualism is true.

It is perhaps significant that none of the standard articles on the Identity theory discuss religious experience except briefly and in passing. Armstrong notes that 'Scientists who still reject the physico-chemical account of man do so primarily for philosophical, or moral or religious reasons.'[93] Crick has 'a strong suspicion that it is the Christians, and the Catholics in particular, who write as vitalists, and that it is the agnostics and atheists who are the anti-vitalists.'[94] Both appear to question the motivation of religious scientists on this issue as if their religious experience were *ipso facto* irrelevant. It may be, however, that religious experience provided additional data which they had to take into account in framing their hypothesis, which was not an illegitimate intrusion of religious dogmatism. To those who have enjoyed such experience, this is valid datum. To those who have not, or who believe that psychological or phenomenological inquiry can show the experience as illusory, this alleged experience is of no evidential value, but might possibly scrape in on the coat tails of telepathy. The evidence on which I rest my case is telepathy; mystical experience is mentioned simply as a more common, though less evidential, variant of telepathy. On empirical grounds, therefore, I argue for a dualist understanding of man as against the Identity hypothesis. In the next chapter I shall investigate the epistemological grounds for dualism.

# 8 Why Materialism is a Self-refuting Theory

Identity theorists expect that future scientific research will establish their hypothesis. In my last chapter I gave my reasons for doubting that their expectations would be fulfilled. I now argue that even if apparently convincing evidence were to be produced in favour of the identity hypothesis, the theory could not possibly be established, for the very act of producing the evidence would suffice to demonstrate its falsity. As an ancient Hindu manual puts it, 'That which enables me to say "I have no soul", is itself the soul'[1]

Let us put this suggestion to the test by examining Hammond's arguments for identifying consciousness with brain-processes: 'The changes in the human brain, including those which are accompanied by consciousness, are essentially physical changes. All conscious processes must therefore be due to antecedent physical changes ... conscious processes must therefore either be the introspective concomitants of the corresponding brain processes, or else (which seems more probable) they must themselves be generated by, and therefore really consist of, the accompanying brain-process.'[2]

The difficulty of this argument is to know what meaning to attach to the word 'therefore' in the context, for the word 'therefore' implies a conscious logical transition of thought — it is not appropriate to use it to describe a mere sequence of physical processes. Hammond wishes us to treat his statements as the reasoned arguments of a responsible agent; but if his conclusions were valid this is just what we could not do. Sir Cyril Burt explains: 'If the whole sequence of statements were indeed merely the effect of a causal chain of physical processes, all blindly and mechanically determined, it would follow that the speaker could not help saying what he did; and his arguments, as reasoned arguments, could carry no weight. Why then should we take the smallest notice of what he says?'[3]

My first response to this argument was to think 'Why not?' After all, the conclusions reached by my Volkswagen Service Station's Diagnostic Machine are 'merely the effect of a casual chain of physical processes all blindly and mechanically determined', and the machine cannot help finding what it does; yet I take the greatest notice of what it finds. Further, Francis Crick reports[4] that a machine programmed to prove various theorems of Euclid has come up with a new proof, so simple that no one had previously noticed that the theorem could be proved in this way. I suggest that no one would seek to refute the validity of this proof simply on the grounds that it has been discovered by a physically determined mechanical system. As J.J.C. Smart points out, we decide whether or not an argument proves what it sets out to prove by considering its internal validity, not by finding out whether it was the product of a programmed machine or a free human agent.[5] And it is on this consideration that Smart seeks to defend the Identity theory against the charge that it is self-refuting.[6]

However at this point we return once more to Sir Cyril's starting position, because we can only check the validity of our own reasons if we are free agents. A computer can make calculations, check figures, and prove theorems, but it cannot check the validity of its own programming. And if we too are programmed we cannot check the validity of our own theories of knowledge. If our minds are physically determined then we have no way of deciding between the merits of different theories of knowledge, for any conclusions we might come to would merely indicate the nature of our brain's programming and not whether its conclusions were true or false.

Hence I believe that physical determinism falls prey to the same criticisms as any other determinist system, namely that if it could apparently be proved true it would, in that proving, be falsified. As J.R. Lucas says, 'The Marxist who says that all ideologies have no independent validity and merely reflect the class interests of those who hold them can be told that in that case his Marxist views merely express the economic interests of his class, and have no more claim to be adjudged true or valid than any other views.'[7]

By rational thought I mean the sort of thinking involved in such things as 'seeing the point of an argument', 'exercising a value judgement', 'choosing a particular goal' or 'initiating purposive activity.' A rational argument is one in which we ourselves arrange our thoughts in a purposive sequence with the object of making a case for the view we wish to defend, or thinking out a problem and giving what Ramsey calls 'our personal backing'[8] to our cogitation. I mention Ramsey's qualifier concerning 'our personal backing', because I recognise that a very high proportion of intelligent behaviour, and of intelligent thinking, does not fall into the category of rational thinking which I am now describing. Much of our thinking involves calculation, analysis and problem-solving directed towards goals which we have not ourselves personally chosen, but with which we have been confronted in our daily life. It is true that to say of a man 'he has a brain like a computer' is normally to pay a compliment to his power of thought; and this reminds us just how much of our daily thinking is mechanical, automatic and unconscious. Much of our intelligent behaviour is learned behaviour and represents habitual response. It remains true however that what is most distinctive about human thought cannot be regarded as predetermined.

Austin Farrer illustrates this point with reference to scientific inquiry:

> Try turning the scientist's attention on his activity of discourse, and persuading him that he does not frame it in any sense which excludes its being framed by causal factors; does not either ask questions or reply to them, otherwise than as they arise of themselves and elicit their own answers. You will find that he is as unable to think this way about his work, and to get on with it, as a man is to deliberate in the belief that his decision is determined. To experiment, to speculate, to pick the fruitful point for

examination — everyone engaged in such endeavour regards them in practice as free activities ... The whole mass of natural fact as we men have put it together is the product of an enterprise which knows itself as free.[9]

Sir John Eccles has strongly urged that free rational thought is of the essence of scientific investigation, and that free rational assessment of the data produced by scientific experiment is what distinguishes genuine scientific inquiry from 'mere reportage.'[10] He criticises those who have 'The naive belief that science is concerned with the making of scientific observations with the best techniques available and that out of these observations there emerges some coherent story or hypothesis.'[11] His method is to urge first the formulation of a rational hypothesis and then its testing by investigation for 'observations which are published just as observations, without organic relationship to precisely formulated hypothesis are ... scientifically meaningless.'[12] In brief, the initiating of purposive activity, and subsequent conscious reflection and assessment of the data, are crucial for any serious investigation.

I.T. Ramsey has argued that most responsible human decision-making takes into account intangible judgements of value as well as publicly observable facts. For instance an examiner in any subject where there are no prescribed answers would be expected to talk in terms of the 'quality' of the work, as well as such observable factors as its length or subject matter.[13] Equally if a man decided to be a doctor we would be disappointed if his sole motivation were thoughts of financial reward or a pleasant life. We tend to expect prospective doctors to think not only of these things, but also of 'a vocation to medicine.'[14] In marriage we do not expect a young couple to decide on marriage simply by weighing up the advantages of a marital over a single state but rather we look for a devotion either to other which will remain constant, 'for better, for worse, for richer for poorer, in sickness and in health, till death us do part.'[15] In all these examples we are given instances of free human behaviour, which displays its distinctively human and personal quality by going beyond what it is appropriate to describe in causal language alone.

Hence I argue that genuine rational thought, scientific inquiry and responsible human decision-making all depend upon the belief that man is free to make genuine purposive choices and to engage in conscious reflection and assessment. I suggest further that these activities would be impossible if the Brain/Mind Identity theory were true, for the brain, as a physical organism, must be subject to the rules of physics and chemistry. If it were not subject to such laws then there would be no point in putting forward the theory; indeed the principal reason for identifying the brain with the mind is the difficulty of believing that states of consciousness should be the one thing left outside the physicalist picture. As Smart says 'That everything should be explicable in terms of physics except the occurrence of sensations seems to me frankly unbelievable.'[16] It is therefore essential to the Identity theory that the brain is subject to the laws of physics and one of these laws is that physical causes always precede effects and that description of phenomena in terms of final causes is not valid.

If one excludes final causes as explanations of human behaviour then all human thought must be determined by prior efficient causation. This means that the concept of purpose is illusory because purposive action is by definition goal-directed activity. It is no criticism of this argument to point out that machines perform goal-directed actions, that for instance the function of a diagnostic machine is to find out the condition of my car, for the machine's activities are not determined by its hopes for the future but by its construction in the past. The element of purpose in this activity comes from the mechanic who decides to attach my car to the machine in order to find out its condition. It is true that if the Identity theory were correct, we would still perform goal-directed activity in the sense which the diagnostic machine does. But then, like the machine, this activity would be controlled by our past construction through our heredity and our environment, and we should consequently be determined by our past. Our thoughts, too, according to a determinist theory, must be the product of our brain's structure and our past history, and consequently our thinking is a guide, not to what is true, but to our past. As Lucas points out, determinists 'are committed to the view that whether or not determinism is true, they will believe that it is as a result of certain physical variables having had certain values at a certain antecedent time[17] . . . Their saying determinism is true affords us no reason for supposing it is really true, but is to be construed solely as the end product of a physical process . . . Determinism therefore cannot be true, because if it was, we should not take the determinists' arguments as being really arguments but as being only conditioned reflexes.'[18] In seeking to demonstrate their thesis the determinists only reveal its falsity. 'They want to be considered as rational agents arguing with other rational agents; they want their beliefs to be construed as beliefs, and subjected to rational assessment; and they want to secure the rational assent of those they argue with, not a brainwashed repetition of acquiescent patter.'[19] Lucas concludes that 'determinism cannot be true . . . for if it were true, it would destroy the possibility of its being rationally considered and recognised as such. Only a free agent can be a rational one. Reasoning, and hence truth, presupposes freedom just as much as deliberation and moral choice do.'[20]

Jacques Monod occupies an interesting position in this discussion for he is an identity theorist who nevertheless fully accepts the force of the epistemological objection to the theory. Monod believes that 'man is an accident based on chance, and the accident is perpetuated by the necessity of chemical reactions.'[21] He is a staunch supporter of the Identity theory: 'Objective analysis obliges us to see that this seeming duality within us is an illusion.'[22] However he accepts that there is a problem because 'In our understanding, in our intuition of the phenomenon, there is . . . a flagrant epistemological contradiction.'[23] The problem is that 'The cornerstone of the scientific method is the postulate that nature is objective. In other words the systematic denial that "true" knowledge can be reached by interpreting phenomena in terms of final causes — that is to say of "purpose".'[24] He recognises that the 'postulate of objectivity is impossible to demonstrate. For it is obviously impossible to imagine an experiment proving the nonexistence anywhere in nature of purpose, or a pursued end.'[25] Nevertheless, he thinks the postulate of objectivity must be accepted as 'an ethical choice and not a judgement reached from knowledge, since, according to the postulate's own terms, there cannot have been any "true" knowledge prior to this arbitrary choice.'[26]

In other words, in spite of the fact that the denial of purpose involves us in 'flagrant epistemological contradiction', Monod believes we should make an act of will, an 'ethical choice' to look at nature and man without making use of any concept of purpose. This Monod does, explaining the 'teleonomy, or apparent purposiveness, in man as an evolutionary product of chance and necessity, and hence our apparently goal-directed activities are the products of our past evolutionary history and not of our present purposing.'[27] Monod takes up this position in spite of the 'profound epistemological contradiction' which he finds to be 'radically insoluble',[28] because he believes that 'the postulate of objectivity is consubstantial with science, and has guided the whole of its prodigious development for three centuries. It is impossible to escape it, even provisionally or in a limited area, without departing from the domain of science itself.'[29]

I have no wish whatever to question the supremacy of scientific method in establishing questions of fact, and I recognise that a systematic denial of 'purpose' is an important part of scientific methodology. But the correct methodology for one sort of inquiry may not be the right way of investigating another type of problem. It seems thoroughly acceptable that when Monod is pursuing his genetic investigations he should banish all thought of final causes from his mind. But when he comes to write a book, setting forward a universal world view, he has no right to use the same methodology. For in discussing the nature of reality it is impossible to avoid asking the question 'How do we know?'; and if we find ourselves confronted with a 'flagrant epistemological contradiction' we cannot simply make a 'moral choice' to ignore it. It seems the antithesis of all scientific method to decide to ignore data which contradict our own findings. Part of scientific method is to follow facts wherever they may lead.

Although, as we study the world, we find causal sequence to be a universal rule, there are good epistemological grounds for arguing that this rule cannot apply to man's own mind. Monod sees this but ignores it, and his thesis, I suggest, is thereby undermined.

He accepted that no experiment could ever disprove purpose, but has failed to notice that the same applies to any argument purporting to do so.

It may indeed seem odd that we should wish to claim that the human mind alone of all subjects of our inquiry should not be in principle explicable by the laws of physics and chemistry. And yet it seems a necessary condition of our learning these laws that our minds should be free. As Austin Farrer comments, 'if it is true that it is only by a freely-pursued investigation that the determined order of the world is discovered, the fact of universal order can never be more certain than the liberty of the mind which discovers it.'[30] Hence I believe that any materialist theory of mind must be self-refuting and unworthy of our rational allegiance.

# 9 The Immortality of the Soul

In my last three chapters I have sought to establish that in our present lives the mind or soul is a reality which is both logically and contingently distinct from the body, and that indeed it is only on the assumption of such a distinction that we can formulate a valid theory of knowledge. I have attempted to explain the undoubted relationship between mind and body in terms of a two-way interaction in which every physical change affects the mind and every mental change affects the body. But in the light of this one-to-one relationship is it really conceivable that the mind could enjoy any kind of personal life without a bodily frame to give expression to its will, and to provide it with the sensory stimuli for its consciousness?

One answer to this question might be 'no'. This would not rule out the possibility of personal survival, for I argued in Chapter 5 that the expectation of many contemporary Christians that they will receive new and different bodies in a heaven in another space is not an unreasonable hope, in that the idea is internally coherent, its realisation is logically feasible and it would not have bizarre implications. In such a theory the new body would be, *ex hypothesi*, 'an appropriate organ of expression and activity',[1] with which the Cartesian soul could interact in its new and continued life. Whether or not this possible life is likely to be realised is not my present concern. I wish solely to point out that it is a theoretically realisable possibility.

But must a Cartesian soul possess a body if it is to survive as an experiencing self? Certainly there is a strong *prima facie* case for supposing a body to be necessary for any experiencing. As Professor H.H. Price points out, 'In a disembodied state, the supply of sensori stimuli is perforce cut off, because the supposed experient has no sense organs and no nervous system. There can therefore be no sense perception. One has no means of being aware of material objects any longer; and if one has not, it is hard to see how one could have any emotions or wishes either. For all the emotions and wishes we have in this present life are concerned directly or indirectly with material objects, including of course our own organisms and other organisms, especially human ones. In short, one could only be said to have experiences at all if one is aware of some sort of a world.'[2]

However, having posed this problem, Price has done more than anyone else to provide a possible answer, and it is clear from the writings of Hick,[3] Aldwinckle,[4] Lewis,[5] Ducasse,[6] Penelhum[7] and Flew[8] that his attempt is at the forefront of contemporary debate about the possibility of disembodied existence.

The starting point for Price's Hypothesis is that sense-perception is not necessary for all experiencing. When we dream 'sensory stimuli are cut off . . . but we still manage to have experiences. It is true that sense perception no longer occurs, but something sufficiently like it does. In sleep, our image-producing powers, which are more or less inhibited in waking life by a continuous bombardment of sensory stimuli, are released from this inhibition. And then we are provided with a multitude of objects of awareness, about which we employ our thoughts and towards which we have desires and emotions.'[9] I believe that Price is right in saying that when we dream we undergo real experiences. As H.D. Lewis says, 'We would not be so terror-stricken during a nightmare did we not take all that seems to happen with the utmost serious-ness; it is not, as a rule at least, like watching a horror-film which we know full well is nothing but a film. We do not normally doubt that what seems to happen in a dream is actually taking place.'[10]

Professor Gilbert Ryle has strongly challenged this view, arguing that what we see in our dreams or imagination can in no way be compared to the visual sensations given to us through sense-perception. Naturally he recognises that, figuratively speaking, we do 'see' things in our mind's eye,[11] but he insists that such picturing 'so far from having, or being akin to having, visual sensations, is compatible with having no such sensations and nothing akin to them. There is nothing akin to sensations.'[12] He argues that our very use of language betrays that in practice we are well aware of this difference, for when considering the objects of recollection and imagination we tend to put the words 'see' or 'hear' in inverted commas.[13] Moreover 'a person who says that he "sees" the home of his childhood is often prepared to describe his vision as "vivid", "faithful", or "lifelike", adjectives which he would never apply to his sight of what is in front of his nose . . . In other words, when a person says he "sees" something which he is not seeing, he knows that what he is doing is something which is totally different in kind from seeing . . . The fact that he fails to recognise that he is not seeing, but only "seeing", as in dreams, . . . does not in any way obliterate the distinction'.[14]

Ryle has made two mistakes here. First he has ignored the ambiguity of the verb 'to imagine'. As Price says this can 'sometimes mean "to have mental images". But more usually it means "to entertain propositions without believing them" and very often they are false propositions, and moreover we disbelieve them in the act of entertaining them. This is what happens, for example, when we read Shakespeare's play *The Tempest*, and that is why we say that Prospero and Ariel are "imaginary characters". Mental images are not in this sense imaginary at all. We do actually experience them, and they are no more imaginary than sensations.'[15] In Coleridge's famous phrase, imagination involves the 'willing suspension of disbelief',[16] whereas the images which comes to us in our dreams are quite involuntary, and, for the duration of our dreams, are as objective as the perceptions which we experience in waking life.

Ryle's second error is that he has failed to notice that the only person who really knows what is being experienced is the subject of that experience at the time of the experience. Ryle says 'an imagined shriek is not ear-splitting.'[17] This is certainly true from the point of view of a person sitting by the bed-side of a dreaming subject. But on the assumption that Ryle means 'ear-splitting' only as a synonym for 'loud', it cannot be true for that subject's experience of it during the dream, even though he may on awaking say 'Thank goodness it was only a dream.'

I conclude therefore that it is valid as a starting point to say that dreams show that we can have experiences without sense-perceptions. From this basis Price goes on to suggest that the 'Next world, if there is one, might be a world of mental images.'[18] H.D. Lewis has summed up Price's description of it as:

> an image world, very like the world of our dreams, but with the additional feature of a more comprehensive and complete correlation of the images involved . . . There would be tactual as well as visual images, auditory images and smell images too. There would be images of organic sensations, including somatic sensations connected with the images that would make up one's own body. Such a family of inter-related images would make a pretty good object.[19]

In short, as Price says, it would be a world where

> imagining would perform much the same function as sense-perception performs now, by providing us with objects about which we would have thoughts, emotions and wishes. There is no reason why we should not be 'as much alive', or at any rate feel as much alive, in an image world as we do now in this present material world, which we perceive my means of the sense-organs and nervous systems. And so the use of the word 'survival' [life after death] would be perfectly justifiable.[20]

This theory of a mental existence solves the problem of the whereabouts of the other world for, as I argued in my summary of Quinton's views in Chapter 4, the entities within my dreams are spatially related to each other, but are not at any distance nor in any direction from where I am sleeping. Consequently I believe that Price is right to conclude that 'An image-world would have a space of its own. We could not find it anywhere in the space of the physical world, but this would not prevent it being a spatial world all the same. If you like, it would be its own "where"'.[21]

Although in many respects we would experience a world of images as being closely akin to our present perceptual world, there would be several important differences. According to Price we

> might discover in time that these image-bodies were subject to rather peculiar causal laws. For example, it might be found that in an image-world our wishes to go to Oxford might be immediately followed by the occurrence of a vivid and detailed set of Oxford-like images; even though at the moment before, one's images had resembled Piccadilly Circus ... In that case, one would realise that 'going somewhere' — transferring one's body from one place to another — was a rather different process from what it had been in the physical world.[22]

The inhabitants of this next world would soon learn that

> the causal laws of an image-world would be different from the laws of physics ... [but] by attending to the relations between one image and another, and applying the ordinary deductive method by which we ourselves have discovered the causal laws of this present world in which we live, they too could discover in time what the laws of their world are. These laws, we may suppose, would be more like the laws of Freudian psychology than the laws of physics.[23]

The reason for this difference between our present world and the hypothetical 'next world' would be that a world of images would be essentially mind-dependent, 'presumably in the same way as dreams are now. It would be dependent on the memories and the desires of the persons who experienced it. Their memories and their desires would determine what sort of images they had. If I may put it so, the "stuff" or "material" of such a world would come in the end from one's memories, and the "form" of it from one's desires.'[24]

As can be seen from the vacillation between singular and plural in the above quotations there is a tension in Price's thought between the view they each person would shape his own image-world and the notion that like-minded persons could share a common image-world. This vacillation can be seen throughout his article. At times he suggests that the image-world would be entirely plastic to the individual as in the case above of a man switching his interest, and therefore his image-world, from Piccadilly to Oxford. At other times he argues that 'An image-world such as I am describing would not be the product of one single mind only, nor would it be purely private. It would be the joint-product of a group of telepathically-interacting minds and public to all of them ... there would be many next worlds, a different one for each group of like-minded personalities.'[25]

Professor John Hick has pointed out that it is not easy to combine these two suggestions, 'for desires inhere in individuals, and at the level of ordinary everyday wishes, at any rate, it may be presumed that no two individuals' and certainly no large community of persons' desires coincide sufficiently to be able to be fulfilled in identically the same state of affairs.'[26] He points out that even a devoted husband and wife on holiday might well have differing desires: 'one of them might wish for a calm sea for bathing, the other for tremendous waves for surfing; she might ... wish she were in a dress shop in Paris, whereas he would be disconcerted by her sudden disappearance to fulfill that wish ... But if it is hard to suppose an exact, continuous and detailed correlation of desires even between two individuals who are harmoniously related to one another, it becomes virtually impossible to suppose such a correlation between great multitudes of miscellaneous people populating one and the same world.'[27]

I think this argument is sound, and that Price is in fact trying to hold together in one theory two mutually incompatible ideas of how a mental world can be supposed to function. I suggest that his basic idea can be developed in one of two ways. We might suggest that there are as many private worlds as there are thinking souls, each one plastic to the mind of its thinker. Alternatively we might postulate with Hick one single common world 'whose character is the resultant of the emotions, desires, and memories of the entire human race.'[28] This latter view could, as Hick suggests, be modified to the notion of a hierarchy of different common worlds each suited to a person's spiritual or cultural development. But there could be no precise correlation of any common world to the wishes of any specific individual in it. The notion of a common world and the notion of a world plastic to an individual's desire are mutually exclusive.

Let us consider first the notion of a common world which has a purely mental existence. According to Hick 'we should have to say of such a world that it exists in its totality in the divine consciousness, whilst different parts and aspects of it are imparted to the minds of individual men and women according to the perspectives which they severally occupy within it.'[29] Such a world might in fact be experienced as being identical in structure to our present world, for such an account of the possible next world is closely akin to the account Berkeley gave of the world we now inhabit. Berkeley's account is not generally believed to be true, but it seems accepted that it does justice to our experiencing, and that it is extraordinarily hard to refute. Professor John Hospers makes it clear that he disagrees with Berkeley. He describes his theory as 'Utterly absurd and utterly irrefutable',[30] and he ends his section with the plaintive plea 'But how on earth can [his argument] be attacked!'[31] Bertrand Russell says 'for one who believes in mental substance, as Berkeley does, there is no valid means of refuting it.'[32] As to the relative validity of Berkeley's position, Russell states at the end of his chapter on Berkeley in his *History of Western Philosophy*, 'I do not at present propose to decide . . . The decision, if possible at all, can only be made by an elaborate investigation of non-demonstrative inference and the theory of probability.'[33] F.C. Copleston is critical of Berkeley[34] but he agrees that his views on the nature of reality 'were in point of fact quite consonant with common sense.'[35]

I conclude from this that since Berkeley's account of the world is regarded as true to our experiencing and only capable of refutation by highly sophisticated arguments, it follows that a Berkelian next world could provide a suitable world for human souls to resume life in new bodies. These bodies would, *ex hypothesi*, be radically different in reality from our present bodies, but there would be nothing in our experiencing to suggest this to us. This hypothesis could re-habilitate Hick's theory of another world rejected as implausible in Chapter 4. My case against it was that whereas plural spaces are conceivable, exactly similar psycho-physical ones are not. But there is nothing in that argument against a material world and an experientially identical Berkeleyian world co-existing in separate spaces.

Moreover so long as our image-bodies, as experienced, were sufficiently akin to our present ones to serve as vehicles for the expression of our personality and recognisability, we need not suppose that the two worlds would in fact be identical, for as Hick says,

> There is no reason why such a world or series of worlds should be limited in content to the images stored up in the men's memories of their earthly lives, or in its formative principle to the range of present human desires. Its possibilities would be 'open-ended'; and this is perhaps an advantage in such a theory. For it can then accommodate the religious sense that there are vast depths of reality totally beyond our present range of experience: 'as it is written, Eye hath not seen nor ear heard, neither hath it entered into the heart of man, the things which God hath prepared for them that love him.' (1 Cor: 2/9)[36]

The major objection to this theory is that it would seem odd for God to create two worlds in which the mode of human experiencing would appear the same, yet which would involve two radically different ways of being. Hick is aware of this difficulty: 'Given a Berkeleyian account of a post-mortem world (or worlds) we must go on to ask why it should not also apply to our present world, or alternatively why a non-Berkeleyian account should not apply to the next world as well as this.'[37] However, if my arguments in Chapter 4 are valid, the second alternative is closed to us. The first also seems unlikely, for although Berkeley's theory concerning this world is hard to refute, it is harder still to vindicate. The discussion in *Masterpieces of World Philosophy in Summary Form* states: 'Berkeley was thorough and clever in foreseeing and forestalling possible objections. Yet there are criticisms which, while insufficient to prove a diametrically opposite position such as materialism, or even a more moderate realism, nevertheless show that Berkeley's conclusions do not necessarily follow from his premises.'[38] Hence I conclude that to support the notion of a shared existence in a purely mental world one would have to suppose that God created two worlds similar to our experience but totally different in the structure of their being. This hypothesis seems so contrary to Christian belief in God's consistency that I feel it ought to be rejected.

Let us return therefore to the notion of a purely private image-world. Such a world would be subjective in that it would be created out of the desires and memories of the person who thinks it into being, but it would also be objective in the sense that it would be shaped by a man's character, and as Price points out, 'A man's character is... objective in the sense that he has it whether he likes it or not... In the next life, according to my picture of it, it would be these permanent and habitual desires which would determine the nature of the world in which a person has to live. His world would be, so to speak, the outgrowth of his character; it would be his own character respresented to him in the form of dream-like images. There is therefore a sense in which he gets exactly the sort of world he wants... Yet he may very well dislike having the sort of character he does have... Accordingly his image-world is... objective in the sense that it insists on presenting itself to him whether he likes it or not.'[39]

From a Christian point of view there is considerable merit in this part of Price's hypothesis, for it has always been an important element in Christian belief that 'A man reaps what he sows. If he sows seed in the field of his lower nature, he will reap from it a harvet of corruption, but if he sows in the field of the Spirit, the Spirit will bring him a harvest of eternal life.'[40] Moreover the New Testament has also taught that this judgement would be associated with self-knowledge! 'Then shall I know even as I am known'.[41] We will be confronted with ourselves as we truly are: 'Now we only see puzzling reflections in a mirror, but then we shall see face to face'.[42] Price's suggestion therefore links both these New Testament doctrines.

John Hick brings out very clearly the suitability of such an hypothesis for the two ideas of judgement and reformation in the life beyond the grave.

The principle of judgement, or, in Eastern terms, karma, which has been largely postponed in its operation in our present life by a material world which is not immediately responsive to our desires, now comes fully into operation. Our earthly life, completed by death, judges itself by producing an environment for the next stage of our existence which is determined by the quality of our character at the time of death. In general and for most of us that next stage will be purgatorial. For as our desires are uninhibitedly fulfilled their true value will be revealed to us, and in many cases we shall become profoundly dissatisfied with the world which we have made for ourselves. For frequently our dominating desires are extremely trivial from the point of view of richness of emotional and intellectual content, so that their unlimited fulfilment must lead to the terrible accidie of boredom . . . However, if the self-created world which fulfils an individual's wishes is to him hellish rather than heavenly, it may thereby work for his salvation. For it may sooner or later evoke in him a yearning for something better, a longing for a more valuable and ultimately more satisfying existence. He may begin to 'hunger and thirst after righteousness'[43]; and then his desire will lead him on into higher worlds and perhaps finally to a total purification from evil desire and a final entry into the conscious presence of infinite goodness. This will be eternal life, the life of the Kingdom of God, supervening upon a long and perhaps arduous approach both in this world and in the world to come.[44]

But it has been objected that a private world must be a solipsistic one and this goes completely against the Christian belief in the 'Communion of Saints' in a social heaven. Moreover from a totally secular standpoint the idea of an eternal solitary confinement, wrapped up for ever in one's own thoughts, is a horrific notion.

Terence Penelhum writes 'In the Next World as we have now described it the survivor could perceive no thing or person whatever. This does not mean that he could not have, among the images in his experience, images "of" other persons, but whatever they could come to mean to him they could not be perceptions of other disembodied survivors, since those survivors could have no perceptible characteristics . . . Smith's mind may contain images of Jones, but it cannot contain Jones himself.'[45]

To meet this objection H.H. Price argues that

> 'meeting' of a kind might be possible between discarnate experients . . . A special sort of telepathy would be needed; the sort which in this life produces telepathic apparitions. It would not be sufficient that A's thought or emotions should be telepathically affected by B's. If such telepathy were sufficiently prolonged and continuous, and especialy if it were reciprocal, it would indeed have some of the characteristics of social intercourse — but I do not think we should call it 'meeting' . . . It would be necessary, in addition, that A should be aware of something which could be called B's body, or should have an experience not too unlike the experience of seeing another person in this life. The additional condition would be satisfied if A experienced a telepathic apparition of B. It would be necessary, further, that the telepathic apparition by means of which B 'announces himself' . . . should be recognisably similar on different occasions. And if it were a case of meeting some person again whom one had previously known in this world the telepathic apparition would have to be recognisably similar to the physical body which that person had when he was still alive.[46]

I see no reason why one should not accept this part of Price's argument without going on to accept his view that telepathically — interacting minds might shape a common world. Indeed I think that the great virtues of Price's theory would be lost if they did. I suggest that the notion of private mental worlds which possess the capacity for personal communication via telepathy leads not to solipsism, but to quite the contrary. I suggest that only such a hypothesis could enable the fulfilment of what is for many the principal element in the hope for a future life — namely the re-union in heaven with those whom we 'have loved long since and lost awhile.'[47] In a common world there would seem no way the generation gaps could be bridged. I could only recognise my grand-father as a man in his eighties, but his grandfather could only recognise him as a young boy. A young mother who had lost a child of ten might long to see her loved one again, but how could the child recognise as his mother the woman of eighty who had just arrived in the resurrection world? Moreover we are living in an age of increasing transcience and rootlessness. In the last twelve years I have lived in Reading, Windsor, Oxford, Petersfield, Cambridge, Birmingham, and now Lampeter. If I arrived in a resurrection world tomorrow among which grouping of people would I be placed for re-union to happen? Moreover, take the classic Sadducean question of the much-widowed woman;[48] in what resurrection-world could she live? Such questions may be intractable but I suggest that the only hypothesis which comes anywhere near a possible answer is that of H.H. Price. For in a private world with telepathic interactions we could each image the people known to us as we had known them, and thus I could communicate with my grandfather and image him as a man of eighty, while my great-great-grandfather could image him as a child of ten, though perhaps in process of time telepathic interaction would enable us both to move toward a common image.

There would remain a temporary solipsistic stage in the experiencing of the recently departed whose thoughts and desires might well create an image-world comprised largely of persons still living with whom telepathic interaction would be unusual, though in the light of the evidence discussed in Chapter 2, not unknown. This solipsistic period would be necessary for the process of reflection and self-judgement on our earthly life which I suggested earlier would be the first step in our future development. Thereafter we would expect telepathic interaction with other deceased persons and religious experience of God to move our thoughts away from their initial solipsistic concern for the persons left behind who would of course ultimately join us yonder.

A second virtue of Price's theory is that it seems the only hypothesis of a future life which can take into account the data provided by the resurrection appearances of Jesus. In chapter 2 I argued that these can 'best be understood as veridical hallucinations, revealing truthfully the fact of Jesus' continued aliveness to the disciples' minds.' I suggested that 'the source of this information was Jesus himself, communicating telepathically to his disciples.' If this argument is valid, and if Price's hypothesis seems reasonable, then we might suggest that Christ's resurrection appearances to his disciples instance the way all of us would communicate with each other in the next world.

I suggest that any other theory of a next world must discard the data provided by the resurrection of Jesus. For if my arguments in earlier sections of this book are valid, then we can no longer think of Christ's resurrection as the prelude to corporeal ascension to a heaven in the sky, nor can we regard it as the harbinger of what may happen to our bodies at the end of time; nor should we describe it as a 'spiritual body', for I have argued that such a notion is a logical hybrid. On the other hand I have defended the notion that the resurrection was a real event open to historical inquiry, and hence provides relevant data for us to take into account in the formulation of our theories about reality.

A third virtue of Price's theory is that it can do justice to the Christian conviction that in the next world God will be much more real to us that He is in our present existence. If I was right in Chapter 7 to suggest that religious experience and telepathy are analogous, then we would expect that just as our powers of telepathic communication would be enhanced in a purely mental existence, so too would be the quality of our religious experiencing. Since claimed religious experience of God is much more common in this life than claimed telepathic rapport with other minds, we might suppose that when both ways of experiencing come fully into their own in the next life, religious experience would retain its relative dominance. Hence God would become the most vital subject of our awareness. This would exactly tie in with the belief that the 'beatific vision' is to be the most significant element in the life of heaven.

Moreover, the view that our relationship with God would be enhanced in the next world reminds us that one of the primary theological grounds for believing in a future life is the conviction that in this life we can enter into a relationship with God which death cannot sever. We noticed in Chapter 1 how important this feeling was to the movement in Old Testament thought towards a future hope.

I conclude therefore that Price's theory of a purely mental existence is logically possible and internally coherent, that it satisfies the Christian belief in divine justice, and the hope that we may progress toward fullness of life in the world beyond. It allows for a social understanding of a future life, it takes into account the data provided by the resurrection appearances of Jesus, and it helps to explain the concept of the beatific vision. Moreover, although within the Christian tradition this theory is relatively new, it would not provide a bad fulfilment for much earlier Christian thinking. Consider Peter Abelard's vision of heaven in his hymn for Saturday vespers:

> Truly 'Jerusalem' name we that shore,
> 'Vision of peace', that brings joy evermore!
> Wish and fulfilment can severed be never,
> Nor the thing prayed for come short of the prayer.[49]

This argument does not prove that the soul is necessarily immortal. All that I would wish to claim for this hypothesis of a purely mental existence, and for the hypothesis in Chapter 5 about re-embodiment in heaven, is that they show that it is still possible to spell out the Christian hope in ways that are reasonable, in the sense that we can conceive their possibility without having to contradict other well-established beliefs that we may have about the world and about human existence.

# Notes

*Chapter 1*
1. 2 Samuel 14/14.
2. Job 20/7.
3. Genesis 2/7, 3/19; Job 10/9, 34/15; Psalms 90/3, 103/14, Ecclesiastes 3/20.
4. Isaiah 14/11.
5. E. C. Rust, *Nature and Man in Biblical Thought* (Lutterworth, 1953) p. 104.
6. Genesis 35/18.
7. Ecclesiastes 12/7.
8. E. Jacob, *Theology of the Old Testament* (Hodder, 1955) p. 160; W. Eichrodt, *Theology of the Old Testament*, II (SCM, 1967); A. R. Johnson, *The Vitality of the Individual in the Thought of Ancient Israel* (Cardiff, 1964).
9. Eichrodt, *Theology of the Old Testament*, II, p. 47.
10. Genesis 6/17, 7/15; Ecclesiastes 3/19.
11. Genesis 2/7; Job 33/4.
12. Genesis 6/3.
13. Psalm 104/29; Job 34/14—15.
14. Ecclesiastes 12/7.
15. Eichrodt, *Theology of the Old Testament*, II, p. 135.
16. Genesis 35/18.
17. Ecclesiastes 3/19.
18. Psalms 90/5, 103/15; Isaiah 40/7; Job 14/2.
19. Job 14/1—19.
20. Psalm 146/4.
21. Ecclesiastes 9/5—6.
22. R. H. Charles, *Eschatology* (Schocken, 1963) p. 32.
23. Ibid., p. 33.
24. Ibid., p. 53.
25. A. Weiser, *The Psalms* (SCM, 1963) pp. 389—90; G.W. Anderson in M. Black and H. H. Rowley, *Peake's Commentary* (Nelson,1963) p. 416; H. Wheeler Robinson, *Inspiration and Revelation in the Old Testament* (OUP, 1962) p. 102.
26. Job 12/10.
27. Genesis 5/22—5; 2 Kings 2/11.

28. Genesis 5/24; Hebrews 11/5.

29. 1 Kings 19/12.

30. E. W. Heaton, *The Old Testament Prophets* (Penguin, 1969) pp. 44—5.

31. 1 Kings 18/22, 19/10, 19/14.

32. Heaton, *Old Testament Prophets*, p. 82

33. Charles, *Eschatology*, pp. 59—60.

34. Jeremiah 31/27.

35. H. Cunliffe-Jones, *Jeremiah* (SCM, 1960) p. 199; B. W. Anderson, *The Living World of the Old Testament* (Longman's, 1964); J. Paterson in *Peake's Commentary*, p. 556; N. K. Gottwald, *A Light to the Nations* (Harper, 1959) p. 370

36. Jeremiah 4/4, 9/26.

37. Jeremiah 8/8—13.

38. Jeremiah 12/2, 7/21—8, 6/20, 11/15.

39. Jeremiah 7/14.

40. Heaton, *Old Testament Prophets*, p. 80.

41. Charles, *Eschatology*, p. 61.

42. Ibid., p. 64.

43. Ezekiel 18/20.

44. Psalm 34/10.

45. Psalm 37/9.

46. Psalm 91/9—10.

47. Proverbs 13/2.

48. Proverbs 13/25.

49. Proverbs 11/8.

50. Herbert Butterfield, *Christianity and History* (G. Bell, 1949).

51. Ibid., p. 49.

52. Ibid., pp. 49—50.

53. Proverbs 11/18.

54. Proverbs 22/8.

55. Ecclesiastes 7/15.

56. Job 21/17.

57. Job 21/7—13.

58. Ecclesiastes 9/2—3.

59. Job 42/3.

60. John Hick, *Evil and the God of Love* (Macmillan, 1966) 374—6.

61. Ecclesiastes 2/20. In the preceding verses Ecclesiastes explains that it is the inevitability of death which gives rise to this despair. In 3/19—22 he seems to reject belief in a future life on the grounds that it is something for which there is no evidence. He does not explicitly deny the possibility, but the whole tone of his thought is against it: cf. 5/15—19, 6/4—6 and especially 9/3—6 which concludes, 'The dead know nothing. There are no more rewards for them; they are utterly forgotten. For them love, hate, ambition, all are over. Never again will they have any part in what is done here under the sun.'

62. Job 14/13—19.

63. Charles, *Eschatology*, p. 71.

64. William Irwin in the 1962 *Peake's Commentary*, p. 399.

65. Charles, *Eschatology*, p. 71.

66. T. H. Robinson, *Job and his Friends* (SCM, 1954) p. 101.

67. H. H. Rowley, *From Moses to Qumran* (Lutterworth, 1963) pp. 181–2.

68. Job 7/6 RSV; cf. the NEB translation: 'My days are swifter than a shuttle, and come to an end when the thread runs out.'

69. Eichrodt, *Theology of the Old Testament*, II, p. 509.

70. J. Bright, *A History of Israel* (SCM, 1962) p. 439.

71. Job 10/8.

72. Job 10/10–13.

73. Job 31/18. This interpretation of the verse occurs only in the Jerusalem Bible translation, but the same sentiment occurs in Job 29/2–3.

74. Job 23/11–12.

75. Job 7/21.

76. Ecclesiastes 3/19.

77. Ecclesiastes 9/1.

78. Ecclesiastes 2/11, 2/17 and passim.

79. Ecclesiastes 3/11.

80. Ecclesiastes 3/13.

81. Ecclesiastes 3/22.

82. Ecclesiastes 9/9.

83. Ecclesiastes 6/9.

84. John Hick, *Christianity at the Centre* (SCM, 1968) p. 58.

85. D. S. Russell, *Method and Message of Jewish Apocalyptic* (SCM, 1971) p. 356.

86. Psalm 16/9–11.

87. Weiser, *The Psalms* p. 176.

88. Ibid., p. 178.

89. G. W. Anderson in the 1962 *Peake's Commentary*, p. 416, para 364 b.

90. Psalm 49/12 & 20.

91. Psalm 49/15.

92. Charles, *Eschatology*, p. 75.

93. Psalm 49/15 RSV ('Take me', NEB).

94. Weiser, *The Psalms*, p. 389.

95. Wheeler Robinson *Inspiration and Revelation in the Old Testament*, p. 102.

96. Gottwald, *A Light to the Nations*, p. 511.

97. Psalm 73/23–8.

98. Charles, *Eschatology*, p. 77.

99. Weiser, *The Psalms*, p. 514.

100. Eichrodt, *Theology of the Old Testament*, II, p. 525–6.

101. Wheeler Robinson, *Inspiration and Revelation in the Old Testament*, p. 103.

*Chapter 2*

1. 1 Corinthians 15/1–2.

2. W. Neil, *The Life and Teaching of Jesus* (Hodder, 1963) p. 153.

3. A. M. Ramsey, *The Resurrection of Christ* (Fontana, 1963) p. 10.

4. Hebrews 11/5; 2 Kings 2/11; cf. 'Assumption of Moses' in F. L. Cross, *Oxford Dictionary of Christian Church*.

5. 1 Corinthians 15/22.

6. C. F. D. Moule, *The Significance of the Message of the Resurrection for Faith in Jesus Christ* (SCM, 1968) p. 118.

7. Ibid., p. 115.

8. Ibid., p. 114.

9. Ibid., p. 117.

10. G. Bornkamm, *Jesus of Nazareth* (Hodder, 1966) p. 9.

11. D. M. Mackinnon, *The Borderlands of Theology* (Lutterworth, 1968) p. 76.

12. Moule, *Significance of the Resurrection*, p. 113.

13. H. W. Bartsch, *Kerygma and Myth* (Harper, 1961) p. 42.

14. H. Zahrnt, *The Historical Jesus* (Collins, 1963) p. 125.

15. Ibid., p. 132.

16. Ibid., p. 132.

17. Moule, *Significance of the Resurrection*, p. 25.

18. Ibid., p. 31.

19. Ibid., p. 17.

20. *Encyclopaedia Britannica*, II 341.

21. (Cormarket Press, 1969) p. 238.

22. *Annals* 15/442–8 in J. Stevenson, *A New Eusebius* (SPCK, 1963) p. 2.

23. Origen, *Contra Celsum* 2/12 (OUP, 1965) p. 77.

24. C. H. Dodd, *The Founder of Christianity* (Collins, 1971) P. 11.

25. Sura 4/–57; cf. S. Neill, *Christian Faith and Other Faiths* (OUP, 1971) p. 63.

26. D. E. Jenkins & G. B. Caird, *Jesus and God* (Faith Press, 1965) p. 9–15.

27. H. Montefiore, *Sermons from Great St Mary's* (Fontana, 1968) p. 158.

28. John 20/19.

29. D. Cupitt, *Christ and the Hiddenness of God* (Lutterworth, 1971) p. 138.

30. Ibid., p. 141.

31. cf. Acts 2/32, 10/40.

32. Bartsch, *Kerygma and Myth*, p. 38.

33. Ibid., p. 41.

34. Matthew 27/46; Mark 15/34.

35. G. W. H. Lampe and D. M. Mackinnon, *The Resurrection* (Mowbrays, 1966) p. 9.

36. Neil, *Life and Teaching of Jesus*, p. 153.

37. Bartsch, *Kerygma and Myth*, p. 42.

38. 1 Corinthians 15/3–8.

39. Lampe and Mackinnon, *The Resurrection*, p. 36; Moule, *Significance of the Resurrection*, p. 26.

40. cf.Acts 9/3–8; 22/6–11; 26/12–15. Lampe and Mackinnon, *The Resurrection*, pp. 8, 36.

41. Matthew 28/2–10.

42. Matthew 28/17.

43. Luke 24/1–31.

44. Luke 24/36–50.

45. John 20/14–17.

46. John 20/19–29.

47. John 21/4.

48. Galatians 1/15.

49. Bartsch, *Kerygma and Myth*, p. 42.

50. Moule, *Significance of the Resurrection*, p. 61.

51. Lampe and Mackinnon, *The Resurrection*, p. 38.

52. Moule, *Significance of the Resurrection*, p. 6.

53. Lampe and Mackinnon, *The Resurrection*, p. 39.

54. Ramsey, *The Resurrection of Christ*, p. 50.

55. Ibid., p. 50.

56. Lampe and Mackinnon, *The Resurrection*, p. 39.

57. Acts 9/5, 22/8, 26/15; 1 Corinthians 9/1, 15/8.

58. B. H. Streeter, *Foundations* (Macmillan, 1912) p. 134.

59. Ibid., p. 136.

60. Ibid., p. 136.

61. M. Perry, *The Easter Enigma* (Faber, 1969) pp. 188–96.

62. G. N. M. Tyrell, *Apparitions* (Duckworth, 1953) p. 77.

63. Ibid., p. 79.

64. Ibid., p. 54.

65. John 20/19.

66. Luke 24/31.

67. Luke 24/51; cf. Acts 1/9.

68. Matthew 28/17.

69. John 20/17.

70. Perry, *The Easter Enigma*, p. 148.

71. *Macbeth*, Act 3, Sc. 4; *Julius Caesar*, Act 4, Sc.3.

72. Perry, *The Easter Enigma*, p. 147.

73. Ibid., p. 141 (with altered tenses).

74. Tyrell, *Apparitions*, p. 35.

75. 1 Corinthians 15/35 ff.

76. Moule, *Significance of the Resurrection*, p. 10.

77. Cupitt, *Christ and the Hiddenness of God*, p. 144.

78. Ibid., p. 148.

79. Luke 24/40.

80. Acts 10/41.

81. John 20/27; cf. Luke 24/40.

82. Moule, *Significance of the Message of the Resurrection*, p. 7.

83. J. A. Baker, *The Foolishness of God* (DLT, 1970) p. 267.

84. SPCK Theological Collections 6, *Historicity and Chronology in the New Testament* (SPCK, 1965) p. 121.

85. J. N. D. Anderson, *The Evidence for the Resurrection* (IVF, 1950) p. 14.

86. 1Corinthians 15/3—4.

87. *Historicity and Chronology in the New Testament*, p. 130.

88. Ramsey, *The Resurrection of Christ*, p. 73; Moule, *Significance of the Resurrection*, p. 7.

89. Lampe and Mackinnon, *The Resurrection*, p. 43.

90. Acts 17/19.

91. *Historicity and Chronology in the New Testament*, p. 131.

92. Acts 17/33—4.

93. Acts 17/18.

94. B. Russell, *History of Western Philosophy* (Unwin, 1961) p. 261.

95. 1 Corinthians 15/50.

96. Lampe and Mackinnon, *The Resurrection*, p. 46.

97. Ibid., p. 46.

98. J. B. Phillips, *The Ring of Truth* (Hodder, 1967) p. 85.

99. *Historicity and Chronology in the New Testament*, p. 122.

100. Ibid., p. 127.

101. Ibid., p. 128.

102. Moule, *Significance of the Resurrection*, p. 9.

103. Baker, *The Foolishness of God*, p. 261.

104. Ramsey, *The Resurrection of Christ*, p. 72.

105. Lampe and Mackinnon, *The Resurrection*, p. 46.

106. One in John 20/1; two in Matthew 28/1; three in Mark 16/1; three named plus others in Luke 24/10.

107. One man in Mark 16/5; two in Luke 24/4; one angel in Matthew 28/5; two in John 20/12; a whole vision of angels in Luke 24/33.

108. Luke 24/36; John 20/19, 20/26.

109. Luke 23/52—3; 24/42—3.

110. Mark 8/12; Matthew 16/4; Luke 11/29.

111. Jacques Choron, *Death and Western Thought* (Collier-Macmillan, 1973) p. 84.

112. *Historicity and Chronology in the New Testament*, p. 131.

113. Acts 23/8.

114. Josephus, *The Jewish War* (Penguin, 1959) p. 374.

115. G. R. Driver, *The Judaean Scrolls* (Blackwell, 1965) p. 75.

116. John 11/24; Moule, *Significance of the Resurrection*, p. 65; Lampe and Mackinnon, *The Resurrection*, p. 57.

117. Choron, *Death and Western Thought*, p. 82.

118. Moule, *Significance of the Resurrection*, p. 9.

119. C. F. Evans, *Resurrection and the New Testament* (SCM, 1970) pp. 28—30.

120. D. S. Russell, *The Method and Message of Jewish Apocalyptic* (SCM, 1971) p. 369.

121. G. W. Buchanan in R. H. Charles, *Eschatology* (Schocken, 1963) viii.

122. Ibid., p. 73.

123. Ibid., p. 72.

124. Russell, *Method and Message of Jewish Apocalyptic*, p. 359.
125. James Barr, *Old and New in Interpretation* (SCM, 1966) p. 52.
126. Mark 12/24, 12/27.
127. Mark 12/25.
128. 1 Corinthians 15/50.
129. Montefiore, *Sermons from Great St Mary's*, p. 160.
130. 1 Corinthians 15/12–19.
131. Lampe and Mackinnon, pp. 58–9
132. 1 Peter 3/18, 4/6.
133. 2 Corinthians 4/14, 5/1.
134. W. Pannenberg, *Jesus – God and Man* (SCM, 1970).
135. Moule, *Significance of the Resurrection*, p. 130.
136. Pannenberg, *Jesus – God and Man*, p. 81; Moule, *Significance of the Resurrection*, p. 129.
137. 1 Corinthians 15/23–4.
138. Pannenberg, *Jesus – God and Man*, p. 66–73.
139. Ibid., p. 87.
140. Lampe and Mackinnon, *The Resurrection*, p. 59.
141. Pannenberg, *Jesus – God and Man*, p. 101.
142. Ibid., p. 87.

*Chapter 3*
NOTE: Patristic works may be found in the *Ante-Nicene Christian Library* (T. & T. Clark, 1872) and in the *Nicene and Post-Nicene Fathers* (Parker, 1900).
1. Rufinus, *Apostle's Creed*, para. 42.
2. Revelation 20/13.
3. Augustine, *City of God* 22/20.
4. Rufinus, *Apostle's Creed*, para. 43.
5. M. E. Dahl, *The Resurrection of the Body* (SCM, 1962) p. 37.
6. Justin, *On the Resurrection*, Ch. 8; Athenagoras, *On the Resurrection*, Ch. 15; Tatian, *To the Greeks*, Ch. 15; Irenaeus, *Heresies* 5/6/1; Tertullian, *Concerning the Resurrection*, Ch. 34; Methodius, *Discourse on Resurrection*, Ch. 4; Archelaus, *Fragment* of in Ante-Nicene Library xx 308; Arnobius, *Against the Pagans*, 2/2; Cyril of Jerusalem, *Lecture* 4, Ch. 18; Augustine, *City of God*, 14/5; Origen, *First Principles* 2/2.
7. Irenaeus, *Heresies* 5/6/1.
8. Athenagoras, *On the Resurrection*, Ch. 15.
9. P. Geach, *God and the Soul* (RKP, 1969) p. 22.
10. Tertullian, *Concerning the Resurrection*, Ch.34.
11. Jerome, *To Pammachius*, para. 31.
12. Athenagoras, *On the Resurrection*, Ch. 17.
13. Ibid., p. 21.
14. Tertullian, *Concerning the Resurrection*, Ch. 14.
15. Rufinus, *Apostle's Creed*, para. 43.
16. John of Damascus, *Exposition of the Faith*, Ch. 27.
17. Tertullian, *Concerning the Resurrection*, Ch. 11.

18. Justin, *On the Resurrection*, Ch. 8.

19. Irenaeus, *Heresies* 5/3/2.

20. Athenagoras, *On the Resurrection*, Ch. 2.

21. Irenaeus *Heresies* 5/15/3.

22. Pseudo-Justin *On the Resurrection*, Ch. 5. Cyril, *Lecture* 18 1/9. Athenagoras, *On the Resurrection*, Ch. 17.

23. Ibid., Ch. 17.

24. cf. Francis Crick, *Of Molecules and Man* (University of Washington, 1966) pp. 31–60.

25. *Octavius*, Ch. 34.

26. Tertullian, *Concerning the Resurrection* Ch. 12. Tatian, *Theophilus to Autolycus* 1/2/53.

27. Tertullian, *Concerning the Resurrection*, Ch. 12.

28. *Octavius*, Ch. 34.

29. *Nisibene Hymn* 65

30. Tertullian, *Concerning the Resurrection*, Ch. 13, *1 Clement* 26 Cyril of Jerusalem, *Lecture* 18, 1/8 Ambrose, Bk 2, *On Belief in the Resurrection*, para. 57. *Apostolic Constitutions*, Bk 5, Ch. 7.

31. Prayer Book numbering. In Tertullian it was 91/13.

32. Tertullian, *Concerning the Resurrection*, Ch. 13.

33. cf. Jerusalem Bible.

34. K. Stendahl, *Immortality and Resurrection* (Macmillan, 1966) p. 95.

35. A.M. Ramsey, *The Resurrection of Christ* (Fontana, 1963) p. 111.

36. *1 Clement* 26.

37. Ezekiel 37.

38. Irenaeus, *Heresies* 5/15/1; Tertullian, *Concerning the Resurrection*, Ch. 29; Cyprian, *Against the Jews*, Bk 3/58; Ambrose, Bk 2, *Belief in the Resurrection*, para 66; John of Damascus, *Exposition of the Faith*, Ch. 27; Aphrahat, *Demonstration* 8; *Nisibene Hymn* 65 Cyril of Jerusalem, *Lecture* 18, 1/15; Methodius, *Discourse on the Resurrection*, Ch. 18.

39. Cited by Methodius in *Discourse on the Resurrection*, Ch. 18.

40. Ibid.

41. cf. article in 1962 *Peake's Commentary*, p. 586.

42. Tertullian, *Concerning the Resurrection*, Ch. 10; Irenaeus, *Heresies*, 5/33/4.

43. cf. C.R. North, *The Second Isaiah* (Oxford, 1964) pp. 16–17.

44. Genesis 27/28–29; Isaiah 11; Ezekiel 34/23–31, 36/26–36; Daniel 7/13–14.

45. cf. 1962 *Peake's Commentary*, pp. 195, 499, 585–6 and 598.

46. Genesis 5/24, Hebrews 11/5; Irenaeus, *Heresies* 5/5/1; Cyprian, *Against the Jews* 3/58; *Apostolic Constitutions* 5/7; Methodius, *Discourse on the Resurrection*, Ch. 14.

47. 2 Kings, 2/11. For Irenaeus, Methodius and the Apostolic Constitutions cf. note 46.

48. Daniel 3; Tertullian, *Concerning the Resurrection*, Ch. 58; Irenaeus, *Heresies* 5/5/2

49. cf. note 46
50. Ibid.
51. cf. Tertullian, *Concerning the Resurrection* Ch. 58.
52. Ibid.
53. Tertullian, *Concerning the Resurrection*, Ch. 31; Irenaeus, *Heresies* 5/15/1; Augustine, *City of God* 20/26.
54. *Apostolic Constitutions* 5/7.
55. Irenaeus, *Heresies* 5/6/1; Tertullian, *Concerning the Resurrection*, Ch. 47.
56. A.E. Harvey, *Companion to the New Testament* (Oxford, 1971) p. 654.
57. Irenaeus, *Heresies* 5/7/1
58. Ibid. 5/6/2. *2 Clement* 9.
59. Jeremiah 7/12.
60. 1 Corinthians 15/50.
61. Mark 12/25.
62. Irenaeus, *Heresies* 5/9/4.
63. Ibid. 5/14/4.
64. Tertullian, *Concerning the Resurrection*, Ch. 50.
65. Ibid., Ch. 51.
66. *Doctrine in the Church of England* (SPCK, 1962) p. 89.
67. Justin, *On the Resurrection*, Ch. 2; Jerome, *Letter* 101, para. 23; Methodius, *Discourse on the Resurrection*, Ch. 10.
68. G. R. Driver, *The Judaean Scrolls* (Blackwell, 1965) p. 75.
69. *Against Heresies* 5/13/1; Mark 5/22 ff., John 11/34 ff., Luke 7/11 ff.
70. *Apostolic Constitutions*, Bk 5 Ch. 7.
71. cf. John 11/43 ff., Luke 16/20 ff.
72. Polycarp, *Epistle* 2; Ignatius, *Trallians*; Justin, *On the Resurrection*, Ch. 9; Irenaeus, *Heresies* 5/7/1; Tertullian, *Concerning the Resurrection*, Ch. 2; *Apostolic Constitutions* 5/7; Cyprian, *Treatise* 7, Ch. 21; Eusebius, *Oration* 15/8; Pamphilius, *Defence of Origen*; Augustine, *City of God* 22/5; Rufinus, *Apostle's Creed*, para 46; Jerome, *Letter* 108, para. 24.
73. cf. J.G. Davies in J.T.S. October 1972. Justin, *Apology*, Ch. 11; Irenaeus, *Heresies* 5/36/1; Tertullian, *Concerning the Resurrection*, Ch. 59.
74. H.W. Bartsch, *Kerygma and Myth* (Harper, 1961) p. 1.
75. Alan Richardson, *Religion in Contemporary Debate* (SCM, 1966) p. 72.
76. Ibid p. 73.
77. For Greek, Latin, German and French cf. Cassell's dictionaries. For Hebrew cf. Young's *Analytical Concordance*.
78. cf. 'Heaven' in the *Shorter Oxford English Dictionary*, 3rd edition.
79. Acts 1/11.
80. cf. Young's *Analytical Concordance*.
81. Eichrodt, *Theology of the Old Testament*, II, Ch. 15, p. 93 ff.

82. Gregory of Nyssa might be a possible exception. He explicitly says that Hades is not a place but a state of being (*On the Soul and the Resurrection* p. 443) and states that God is our locality (p. 452). All other Fathers seem to be talking about a place.

83. Augustine, *City of God*, Vol. 2, 13/18.

84. Ibid. 22/11.

85. Ibid. 13/18, 22/11.

86. Ibid. 22/11.

87. Ibid. 13/18.

88. Ibid. 13/18.

89. Ibid. 22/4.

90. Irenaeus, *Heresies* 5/36/1; Tertullian, *Concerning the Resurrection*, Ch. 23; Cyprian, *Treatise* 6, Ch. 14; Rufinus, *Apostle's Creed*, Ch. 41; Origen, *First Principles* 2/9/6; Arnobius, *Against the Pagans* 2/77.

91. Justin, *On the Resurrection*, Ch. 9; Tertullian, *Concerning the Resurrection*, Ch. 4; Cyprian, *Treatise* 7, Ch. 26; Gregory Thaumaturgos, *A Discourse on all the Saints*; Eusebius, *Church History* 10/4/46; Jerome, *Letter 75*, para 1; Basil, *Letter 5*, para 2; Gregory of Nazianzus, *Panegyric on Caesarius*, para. 21; Ambrose, Bk 2, *Belief in the Resurrection*, Ch. 132; Origen, *First Principles* 2/9/6; Aphrahat, *Demonstration* 8.

92. See p. 59 above.

93. 1 Thessalonians 4/17.

94. Rufinus, *Apostle's Creed*, para. 46.

95. Conflated from Matthew 13/43 and Daniel 12/3.

96. Rufinus, *Apostle's Creed*, para. 46.

97. Zoe Oldenbourg, *The Heirs of the Kingdom* (Collins, 1972).

98. Origen, *First Principles* 2/3/6.

99. Ibid. 2/11/6−7.

100. Ibid. 2/3/7.

101. Rufinus, *Apostle's Creed*, para. 46.

102. Augustine, *City of God* 22/11.

103. Rufinus, *Apostle's Creed*, para. 46.

104. Origen, *Contra Celsum* 6/21. Genesis 28/12−13.

105. See notes 106−9 and: Lactantius, *Divine Institutes* 7/21; Basil, *Letter* 46, para. 5; Justin, *First Apology*, Ch. 8.

106. *Encyclopaedia Britannica*, Vol. 11, p. 320, 1971 edition.

107. *Octavius*, Ch. 35; Augustine, *City of God* 22/11.

108. William Barclay, *The Plain Man Looks at the Apostle's Creed* (Fontana, 1969) p. 222.

109. Hippolytus, *Treatise of Christ and Anti-Christ*, Ch. 65.

110. R. J. Rees, *Background and Belief* (SCM, 1967) p. 48.

111. Origen, *First Principles* 2/10/4−6.


Chapter 4

1. Jerome, *Letter* 84, Ch. 5.

2. Origen, *First Principles* 3/6/6.

3. Origen, *Contra Celsum* 8/51.

4. M. E. Dahl, *The Resurrection of the Body* (SCM, 1962) p. 10.

5. A. M. Ramsey, *The Resurrection of Christ* (Fontana, 1963) p. 112.

6. Ibid., p. 113.

7. Dahl, *Resurrection of the Body*, p. 48.

8. Aquinas, *Summa Theologia*, Qu. 79 a.1 ('same body'); 79. a. 2 (specific, not numerical identity).

9. Ramsey, *Resurrection of Christ*, p. 113.

10. John Hick, *Death and Eternal Life* (Collins, 1976) p. 281. cf. *Faith & Knowledge* (Macmillan, 1957) pp. 180–6; A. Flew, *Body, Mind and Death* (Macmillan, 1964) pp. 270–5. For Wiener see N. Wiener, *The Human Use of Human Beings* (Sphere) p. 91.

11. C. F. Evans, *Resurrection and the New Testament* (SCM, 1970) p. 10.

12. Hick, *Death and Eternal Life*, p. 279.

13. Austin Farrer, *Saving Belief* (Hodder, 1964) p. 145.

14. Hick, *Death and Eternal Life*, p. 279.

15. Anthony Quinton, 'Space and Times', *Philosophy*, xxxvii (April 1962).

16. Hick, *Death and Eternal Life*, p. 279.

17. H. H. Price, 'Survival and the Idea of Another World' in J.R. Smythies, *Brain and Mind* (Routledge and Kegan Paul, 1968) p. 23.

18. Farrer, *Saving Belief*, p. 145.

19. Ibid.

20. John Hick, *Faith and Knowledge* (Macmillan, 1967) p. 63.

21. Ibid.

22. Roland Puccetti, *Persons* (Macmillan, 1968) p. 63.

23. Ibid., p. 71.

24. See articles on 'Astronomy' and on 'Nebula' in *Encyclopaedia Britannica* (William Benton, 1971).

25. Puccetti, *Persons*, p. 73.

26. Hick, *Death and Eternal Life*, p. 280.

27. Ibid., p. 281.

28. Ibid., p. 284.

29. Ibid., p.285.

30. Ibid., p. 290.

31. Adolf Harnack, *What is Christianity?* (Ernest Benn, 1958).

32. William Barclay, *The Plain Man Looks at the Apostles' Creed* (Fontana, 1967) p. 346.

33. Leonard Hodgson, *For Faith and Freedom* (SCM, 1968) I 235.

34. Ibid., II 98.

35. Hick, *Death and Eternal Life*, p. 292.

36. Ibid., p. 294.

37. Ibid.

38. Ibid.

39. Augustine, *Enchiridion* 3/11.

40. Austin Farrer, *Love Almighty and Ills Unlimited* (Fontana, 1966) p. 2.[

41. *New English Dictionary* (Odhams Press Ltd, 1932): definition of 'accident'.

42. The Apostles' Creed, Prayer Book translation.

43. Romans 6/9.

44. Sir John Eccles, *Facing Reality* (Longman/Springer Verlag, 1970). p. 92.

45. Puccetti, *Persons*, pp. 62–7.

46. G. Rattray Taylor, *The Biological Time Bomb* (Panther, 1969) p. 99.

47. Ibid., p. 119.

48. Matthew 19/26.

49. Hick, *Evil and the God of Love* (Macmillan, 1966) p. 360.

50. Ephesians 4/13.

51. 1 Peter 5/10.

52. 2 Corinthians 4/17.

53. Hick, *Evil and the God of Love*, pp. 383–4.

54. Matthew 22/30 (NEB).

55. Justin, *On the Resurrection*, Ch. 3; Clement of Alexandria, *The Miscellanies* 6/6; Hippolytus, *Fragment from Discourse on Resurrection*; Methodius, *Discourse on Resurrection*, Ch. 9; Rufinus, *Apology in Defence of Himself* 1/8; Jerome, *Letter* 108, para 23.

56. Irenaeus, *Heresies* 5/8/2.

57. Tertullian, *Concerning the Resurrection*, Ch. 61.

58. St Augustine, *City of God* 22/24.

59. St Augustine, *Confessions* 8/1.

60. *Marriage, Divorce and the Church*, The Archbishop's Commission on Marriage (SPCK, 1971) p. 14.

61. Ibid., p. 24.

62. David Stafford-Clark, *What Freud Really Said* (MacDonald, 1965) pp. 104–130.

63. *Marriage, Divorce and the Church*, p. 18.

64. Ibid., p. 20.

65. Hick, *Evil and the God of Love* pp. 361, 362.

66. *Marriage, Divorce and the Church*, p. 41.

67. John Hick, *Philosophy of Religion* (Prentice-Hall, 1963) p. 102.

68. David Martin, *A Sociology of English Religion* (Heinemann, 1967) p. 55.

69. John Hick, *The Existence of God* (Macmillan, 1964) p. 16.

70. Romans 8/21.

*Chapter 5*

1. *Doctrine in the Church of England* (SPCK, 1962) p. 209.

2. *A New Catechism* by the Roman Catholic Bishops of the Netherlands (Herder & Herder/Burns & Oates, 1967) p. 479.

3. Ibid., p. 474.

4. *The Supplement to a New Catechism* (Fontana, 1972) pp. 18, 37.

5. Hans Kung, *Infallible?* (Fontana, 1971) p. 18.

6. M. E. Dahl, *The Resurrection of the Body* (SCM, 1962) p. 8.

7. E. J. Bicknell, *The Thirty-Nine Articles* (Longmans, 1955) p. 102. Michael Paternoster, *Stronger than Death* (SPCK, 1972) p. 53.

8. A. M. Ramsey, *The Resurrection of Christ* (Fontana, 1962) p. 113.

9. C. B. Moss, *The Christian Faith* (SPCK, 1957) p. 448.

10. Russell Aldwinckle, *Death in the Secular City* (George, Allen & Unwin, 1972) p. 87.

11. J. A. Baker, *The Foolishness of God* (Darton, Longman and Todd, 1970) p. 286.

12. Aldwinckle, *Death in the Secular City*, p. 88. Hugh Burnaby, *Thinking through the Creed* (Hodder, 1964) p. 88.

13. Hugh Montefiore, *Sermons from Great St Mary's* (Fontana, 1968) p. 159.

14. John Baillie, *And the Life Everlasting* (OUP, 1934) p. 253.

15. Alec R. Vidler, *A Plain Man's Guide to Christianity* (Heinemann, 1936) p. 248.

16. David Winter, *Hereafter* (Hodder, 1972) p. 65.

17. Charles Gore, *The Reconstruction of Belief* (John Murray, 1951) p. 925.

18. Leonard Hodgson, *For Faith and Freedom* (SCM, 1968) II 195.

19. Austin Farrer, *Saving Belief* (Hodder, 1967) p. 140.

20. Ibid., p. 145.

21. Ibid., p. 142.

22. C. B. Moss, *The Christian Faith*, p. 448.

23. *The Dutch Catechism* p. 273.

24. Montefiore, *Sermons from Great St Mary's*, p. 160; Aldwinckle, *Death in the Secular City*, p. 88; Winter, *Hereafter* p. 65.

25. Vidler, *Plain Man's Guide to Christianity*, p. 248. Paternoster, *Stronger than Death*, p. 53.

26. Hodgson, *For Faith and Freedom*, II 195.

27. Aldwinckle, *Death in the Secular City*, p. 87.

28. Gore, *Reconstruction of Belief*, p. 925; Baker, *Foolishness of God*, p. 287.

29. Ramsey, *Resurrection of Christ*, p. 113.

30. Baillie, *And the Life Everlasting*, p. 253.

31. Burnaby, *Thinking through the Creed*, p. 92.

32. Paternoster, *Stronger than Death*, p. 53.

33. *Doctrine in the Church of England*, p. 209; Aldwinckle, *Death in the Secular City*, p. 88.

34. C. F. D. Moule, 'Does the Resurrection of the body mean the survival of the soul?' pp. 151—8 in *Asking them Questions* Part 1, edited by Ronald Selby Wright (OUP, 1972).

35. G. B. Caird, *The Truth of the Gospel* (OUP, 1950) p. 122.

36. William Barclay, *The Plain man looks at the Apostle's Creed* (Fontana, 1969) p. 346.

37. Maurice Carrey in *Concilium* x,no. 6.

38. J. A. Motyer, *After Death* (Hodder, 1965) p. 87.

39. Supplement to *A New Catechism*, pp. 52—53.

40. Moule, *Significance of the Resurrection*, p. 10.

41. J. S. Whale, *Christian Doctrine* (Fontana, 1963) p. 270.

42. O. C. Quick, *Doctrines of the Creed* (Fontana, 1963) p. 270.

43. Aldwinckle, *Death in the Secular City*, p. 38.

44. This is Heinz Zahrnt's summary of Bultmann's position in *The Question of God* (Collins, 1969) p. 218.

45. David L. Edwards, *The Last Things Now* (SCM, 1969) p. 89.

46. Paul Tillich, *The Shaking of the Foundations* (Penguin, 1963) pp. 71—81.

47. Ibid., p. 75. Cf. *Expository Times* (April 1977) pp. 197—202.

48. In R. Selby Wright, *Asking them Questions*, p. 156.

49. Moule, *Significance of the Resurrection*, p. 10.

50. 2 Peter 3/13.

51. Revelation 21/1.

52. *Encyclopaedia Britannica* xx 1073 (1971).

53. Ibid., VI 587.

54. *Everyman's Encyclopaedia* IV 550.

55. Ibid., IX 221.

56. Barclay, *Plain Man looks at the Apostle's Creed*, p. 346; cf. Caird, *Truth of the Gospel*, p. 123.

57. 1 Corinthians 15/35—8.

58. Farrer, *Saving Belief*, p. 144.

59. *The Concise Oxford Dictionary*, 5th ed. (OUP, 1964).

60. Aldwinckle, *Death in the Secular City*, p. 88.

61. Ibid., p. 88; Baker, *Foolishness of God*, pp. 286—7.

62. Vidler, *Plain Man's Guide to Christianity*, p. 248.

63. Ramsey, *Resurrection of Christ*, p. 102.

64. Gore, *Reconstruction of Belief*, p. 925; Winter, *Hereafter*, p. 66.

65. *The Dutch Catechism* p. 473.

66. Moss, *The Christian Faith*, p. 448; Baillie, *And the Life Everlasting*, p. 254.

67. Hodgson, *For Faith and Freedom*, II 195.

68. Vidler, *Plain Man's Guide to Christianity*, p. 250.

69. Winter, *Hereafter*, p. 77.

70. A. M. Ramsey, *Sacred and Secular* (Longmans, 1966) p. 28.

71. cf. V. H. Mottram, *The Physical Basis of Personality* (Penguin, 1964).

72. Paternoster, *Stronger than Death*, p. 53.

*Chapter 6*

1. René Descartes, *Discourse on Method* (Penguin, 1968) p. 54.

2. Ibid., p. 53.

3. A. J. Ayer, *Language, Truth and Logic* (Gollancz, 1964) pp. 46—7.

4. Bertrand Russell, *History of Western Philosophy* (Unwin, 1961) p. 550.

5. F. C. Copleston, *A History of Philosophy* (Image, 1963) IV 106.

6. A. Flew, *Body, Mind and Death* (Macmillan, 1964) p. 189.

7. P. F. Strawson, *Individuals* (Methuen, 1965) p. 95.

8. Walpola Rahula, *What the Buddha Taught* (Gordon Fraser, 1967) p. 26.

9. Strawson, *Individuals*, p. 95.

10. A. J. Ayer, *The Problem of Knowledge* (Penguin, 1964) pp. 46 —7.

11. Descartes, *Discourse on Method*, p. 58.

12. Ibid., p. 54.

13. William Kneale, *On having a Mind* (CUP, 1962) p. 50.

14. Ibid., p. 51.

15. Ibid., p. 52.

16. Ibid., p. 51.

17. Terrence Penelhum, *Survival and Disembodied Existence* (RKP, 1970) p. 86.

18. Peter Geach, *God and the Soul* (RKP, 1969) p. 27.

19. John Hick, *The Resurrection of the Body* (an unpublished paper, 1973).

20. Descartes, *Discourse on Method*, p. 156.

21. Copleston, *History of Philosophy*, p. 106.

22. Flew, *Body, Mind and Death*, p. 28.

23. Gilbert Ryle, *The Concept of Mind* (Penguin, 1966) pp. 47—8.

24. Ibid., pp. 15—17.

25. H. D. Lewis, *The Elusive Mind* (Unwin, 1969) pp. 50—1, 34—5.

26. Ryle, *Concept of Mind*, p. 57.

27. Lewis, *Elusive Mind*, p. 37.

28. Ibid., pp. 31, 43.

29. Descartes, *Discourse on Method*, p. 129.

30. John Hick, *Biology and the Soul* (CUP, 1972) p. 25.

31. *Oxford Dictionary of the Christian Church*, p. 1370.

32. J. N. D. Kelly, *Early Christian Doctrines*, (Black, 1960) p. 345; Augustine, *City of God*, II 22/4
II 22/4.

33. Hick, *Biology and the Soul*, p. 18.

34. Descartes, *Discourse on Method*, p. 138

*Chapter 7*

1. cf. C. V. Borst (ed.), *The Mind/Brain Identity Theory* (Macmillan, 1970); John O'Connor (ed.), *Modern Materialism: Reading on Mind/Body* (Harcourt, Brace & World Inc., 1969); D. M. Armstrong, *A Materialist Theory of Mind* (RKP, 1968).

2. Borst, *Mind/Brain Identity Theory*, p. 35.

3. S. C. Ratner and W. F. Corning, *The Chemistry of Learning* (New York, 1967); F. R. Babich, A. A. Jacobson, S. Bubash and A. Jacobson, 'Transfer of learning to naive rats by injection of

ribonucleic acid extracted from trained rats', *Science* (1965) 149/656; D. E. Cameron and L. Solyam, 'Effects of RNA on Memory', *Geriatrics* (1961) 16/74.

4. Edward de Bono, *The Mechanism of Mind* (Jonathan Cape, 1969) p. 7.

5. W. Grey Walter, *The Living Brain* (Penguin, 1961) p. 185.

6. J. H. Hick, *Biology and the Soul* (CUP, 1972) p. 12.

7. V. H. Mottram, *The Physical Basis of Personality* (Penguin, 1964) p. 71.

8. Francis Crick, *Of Molecules and Men* (Washington, 1966) p. 87.

9. Paul Tillich, *Theology of Culture* (OUP, 1964) pp. 12–16.

10. V. Lossky, *The Mystical Theology of the Eastern Church* (James Clarke, 1957) pp. 217–235.

11. Tillich, *Theology of Culture*, p. 13.

12. Borst, *Mind/Brain Identity Theory*, p. 46.

13. Reader's Digest, *A.A. Book of the Road* (Reader's Digest, 1970), pp. 78–9.

14. Matthew 26/64.

15. A. M. Ramsey, *The Glory of God and the Transfiguration of Christ* (Longmans, Green & Co., 1949) pp. 16–18.

16. Borst, *Mind/Brain Identity Theory*, p. 47.

17. Ibid., p. 48.

18. Ibid., p. 66.

19. Ibid., p. 67.

20. Crick uses this word to demonstrate his disapproval of mentalist theories of mind.

21. Crick, *Of Molecules and Men*, p. 99.

22. Jacques Monod, *Chance and Necessity* (Collins, 1972) p. 148.

23. Ian Barbour, *Issues in Science and Religion* (SCM, 1966) p. 352.

24. J. C. Eccles (ed.), *Brain and Conscious Experience* (Springer-Verlag, 1966).

25. Ibid., p. xv.

26. Ibid., p. 447.

27. Ibid., p. 218.

28. J. C. Eccles, *Facing Reality* (Longmans/Springer-Verlag, 1970).

29. Ibid., p. 115.

30. Ibid., p. 83.

31. Ibid., p. 127.

32. Antony Flew, *Body, Mind and Death* (Macmillan, 1964) p. 1.

33. Crick, *Of Molecules and Men*, p. 98.

34. Borst, *Mind/Brain Identity Theory*, p. 54.

35. Crick, *Of Molecules and Men*, p. 88.

36. Eccles, *Facing Reality*, pp. 75–9.

37. Eccles, *Brain and Conscious Experience*, p. 292.

38. Eccles, *Facing Reality*, p. 76.

39. Eccles, *Brain and Conscious Experience*, pp. 298–313.

40. Eccles, *Facing Reality*, p. 77

41. Ibid., p. 79.

42. Crick, *Of Molecules and Men*, p. 88.

43. Eccles, *Brain and Conscious Experience*, pp. 298—313.

44. Eccles, *Facing Reality*, p. 79.

45. Crick, *Of Molecules and Men*, p. 86.

46. Monod, *Chance and Necessity*, p. 103.

47. Arthur Koestler, *The Roots of Coincidence* (Hutchinson, 1972) p. 19.

48. Crick, *Of Molecules and Men*, p. 98.

49. Koestler, *Roots of Coincidence*, p. 15.

50. Ibid., p. 14.

51. Ibid., p. 15.

52. R. H. Thouless, *Experimental Psychical Research* (Penguin, 1963); C. D. Broad, *Lectures on Psychical Research* (RKP, 1962).

53. L.A. Vasiliev, *Experiments in Mental Suggestion* (Galley Hull Press, 1963).

54. Koestler, *Roots of Coincidence*, p. 22.

55. Ibid., p. 25.

56. Ibid., p. 28.

57. Ibid., p. 23.

58. C. E. M. Hansel, *ESP: A Scientific Evaluation* (Charles Scribners & Sons, 1966).

59. J. Beloff, *The Existence of Mind* (MacGibbon and Kee, 1962) p. 214.

60. Ibid., p. 218.

61. Koestler, *Roots of Coincidence*, p. 15.

62. Ibid., p. 62.

63. Vasiliev, *Experiments in Mental Suggestion*, p. 5.

64. Koestler, *Roots of Coincidence*, p. 16.

65. J. R. Smythies (ed.), *Science and ESP* (RKP, 1967) p. 58.

66. Keith Campbell, *Body and Mind* (Macmillan, 1970) p. 95.

67. Koestler, *Roots of Coincidence*, p. 17; Smythies, *Science and ESP*, pp. 57—60.

68. Ibid., p. 59; cf. Vasiliev, *Experiments in Mental Suggestion*, p. 142.

69. Koestler, *Roots of Coincidence*, p. 14.

70. Borst, *Mind/Brain Identity Theory*, p. 36.

71. Armstrong, *Materialist Theory of Mind*, p. 365.

72. Campbell, *Body and Mind*, p. 91.

73. Smythies, *Science and ESP*, p. 201.

74. Ibid.

75. Campbell, *Body and Mind*, p. 97.

76. Borst, *Mind/Brain Identity Theory*, p. 67.

77. Armstrong, *Materialist Theory of Mind*, p. 362.

78. Ibid., p. 53.

79. Vasiliev, *Experiments in Mental Suggestion*, p. 5.

80. Smythies, *Science and ESP*, p. 252.

81. Ibid., p. 247.

82. Ibid., p. 246.
83. Ibid., p. 202.
84. Ibid.
85. Borst, *Mind/Brain Identity Theory*, p. 36.
86. Armstrong, *Materialist Theory of Mind*, p. 364.
87. Ibid., p. 363.
88. Campbell, *Body and Mind*, pp. 92, 94–6.
89. Lossky, *Mystical Theology of the Eastern Church*, p. 223.
90. Ibid., p. 224.
91. Tillich, *Theology of Culture*, p. 12.
92. Ibid., p. 13.
93. Borst, *Mind/Brain Identity Theory*, p. 67.
94. Crick, *Of Molecules and Men*, p. 26.

*Chapter 8*
1. *Siva-Nana-Bodham: A Manual of Saiva Religious Doctrine*, translated from the Tamil by G. Matthews. This is an exceedingly rare book which I was loaned by Professor R. C. Zaehner over seven years ago. I did not then take down the page reference for this quotation, and am now unable to obtain it.
2. *Common Factor* No. 4 (Autumn 1966) p. 17.
3. Ibid.
4. Crick, *Of Molecules and Men*, p. 77.
5. John O'Connor, *Modern Materialism*, (Harcourt Brace, 1969) p. 69.
6. Ibid., pp. 68–70.
7. J. R. Lucas, *The Freedom of the Will* (OUP, 1970).
8. I. T. Ramsey, *Freedom and Immortality* (SCM, 1971) p. 22.
9. Austin Farrer, *The Freedom of the Will* (Black, 1963) p. 171.
10. Eccles, *Facing Reality* p. 106.
11. Ibid.
12. Ibid., p. 107.
13. Ramsey, *Freedom and Immortality*, p. 35.
14. Ibid., p. 36.
15. Ibid.
16. Borst, *Mind/Brain Identity Theory* p. 54.
17. Lucas, *Freedom of the Will*, p. 115.
18. Ibid.
19. Ibid.
20. Ibid.
21. Jacques Monod, *Chance and Necessity*, from the summary on the inside cover.
22. Ibid., p. 148.
23. Ibid., p. 30.
24. Ibid.
25. Ibid., p. 31.
26. Ibid., p. 163.
27. Ibid., p. 25.

28. Ibid., p. 31.

29. Ibid.

30. Farrer, *Freedom of the Will*, p. 324.


*Chapter 9*

1. *Doctrine in the Church of England* (SPCK, 1962) p. 209.

2. H. H. Price, 'Survival and the Idea of Another World' in J.R. Smythies (ed.), *Brain and Mind* (Routledge and Kegan Paul, 1968) p. 3.

3. Hick, *Christianity at the Centre* p. 110.

4. Aldwinckle, *Death in the Secular City* pp. 97—9.

5. H. D. Lewis, *The Self and Immortality* (Macmillan, 1973) p. 142.

6. C. J. Ducasse, *The Belief in a Life after Death* (Charles C. Thomas, 1961) p. 128.

7. Terence Penelhum, *Survival and Disembodied Existence* (Routledge & Kegan Paul, 1970) p. 47.

8. Smythies, *Brain and Mind*, p. 25.

9. Ibid., p. 4.

10. Lewis, *The Elusive Mind*, p. 131.

11. Ryle, *Concept of Mind*, p. 232.

12. Ibid., p. 252.

13. Ibid., p. 233.

14. Ibid.

15. Smythies, *Brain and Mind*, p.5.

16. *Oxford Dictionary of Quotations* (OUP, 1959) p. 152 ref. 26.

17. Ryle, *Concept of Mind*, p. 237.

18. Smythies, *Brain and Mind*, p. 4.

19. Lewis, *Self & Immortality*, p. 147.

20. Smythies, *Brain and Mind*, p. 6.

21. Ibid., p. 12.

22. Ibid., p. 7—8.

23. Ibid., p. 15.

24. Ibid., p. 17.

25. Ibid., p. 16.

26. John Hick, *Death and Eternal Life*, (Collins, 1976) p. 270.

27. Ibid., p. 271.

28. Ibid., p. 272.

29. Ibid., p. 275.

30. John Hospers, *An Introduction to Philosophical Analysis* (Routledge and Kegan Paul, 1965) p. 402.

31. Ibid., p. 405.

32. B. Russell, *History of Western Philosophy* p. 627.

33. Ibid., p. 632.

34. Frederick Copleston, *A History of Philosophy* (Image Books, 1964) V, Pt. 2 52.

35. Ibid., p. 13.

36. Hick, *Death and Eternal Life*, p. 275.

37. Ibid.

38. Frank N. Magill, *Masterpieces of World Philosophy* (Allen & Unwin, 1961) p. 453.

39. Smythies, *Brain and Mind*, p. 22.

40. Galatians 6/8.

41. 1 Corinthians 13/12 (AV).

42. 1 Corinthians 13/12 (NEB).

43. Matthew 5/6.

44. John Hick, *Christianity at the Centre* p. 112.

45. Penelhum, *Survival and Disembodied Existence*, p. 52.

46. Smythies, *Brain and Mind*, p. 11.

47. J. H. Newman, 'Lead kindly light', *Hymns Ancient and Modern Revised* (W. Clowes, 1950) No. 298.

48. Mark 12/20—3.

49. *Hymns A. & M. Revised* No. 281.

# Reference Index

# Subject Index

# Index of Names